# Pasta

© Naumann & Göbel Verlagsgesellschaft mbH, a subsidiary of
VEMAG Verlags- und Medien Aktiengesellschaft, Cologne
www.vemag-medien.de

Cover photograph: Uwe Ziss, Düsseldorf
Recipes Photography: TLC Fotostudio

General production: Naumann & Göbel Verlagsgesellschaft mbH
Printed in Germany

ISBN: 978-3-625-11472-7

# Pasta

# Contents

# Versatile Pasta

There is so much more to pasta than meets the eye. From long and thin to short and round, whether filled or hollow, in fanciful shapes or plain, everything is possible. This book moves well beyond the common plate of spaghetti, delicious as it is, to explore the entire range of pasta possibilities. In this chapter, discover all sorts of fascinating facts about the preparation and serving of this multi-faceted staple food.

# Pasta—Versatile and Always a Favorite

Pasta is simply irresistible! When Marco Polo brought this delicious dough back to Europe from his travels, as some claim, no one could have predicted the extent to which it would revolutionize the kitchens of Europe. From the simplest of staples—flour, salt, water and a little oil—a fabulous array of pastas has been developed. Whatever your choice, you will also discover that pasta is uncomplicated and quickly prepared. Experiment with it! This collection of pasta recipes ranges from hearty and rustic to light and summery, and is sure to include something for every taste and occasion.

## A brief guide to noodles

"Pasta" means dough, and it has remained quite constant from the beginning of noodle history. The basic ingredients have always been water and flour, wheat flour in the West and often rice or soy flour for Asian noodles. Eggs may be added for aroma and color, as well as herbs and vegetables. The dough is then kneaded, these days usually by large machines, rolled and pressed into shape, or cut, then finally dried.

In preparation, the flour determines the outcome, from pale yellow to dark brown. Whole wheat yields heartier, darker pasta with a higher protein, vitamin, and mineral content. However, pasta made from white flour is not unhealthy and fattening. On the contrary, it is low in fat, has a worthwhile plant protein content of about 15%, and is a good source of fiber. The body breaks down the carbohydrates in pasta gradually in the body, which is how pasta delivers long-lasting energy for physical and mental endeavours. There is a good reason that high-endurance athletes eat a great deal of pasta. Four ounces of uncooked pasta has 350 calories; cooked, about 110 to 120 calories. The true calorie bombs, therefore, are actually sauces laden with cream and cheese.

## Cooking pasta the right way

If pasta is under- or overcooked, not even the most delectable sauce can save it. Give it the proper attention and cook it, as the Italians say, *al dente*, or to the bite.

In order for pasta to come out just right every time, observe the following tips:

- For each portion (about 4–5 oz/100 g) use at least one quart/liter of boiling water

- Because unsalted water boils faster, add the salt after the water begins to boil

- Use a large, deep pot so that during the cooking process the pasta has enough room, and doesn't stick together

- Adding (olive) oil to the pot is not necessary, but a matter of taste. Stirring will help prevent the pasta from sticking

- Put pasta into boiling water. Stand large noodles in the pot and let them slide in

- Cook the pasta in boiling water in an uncovered pot and be sure to stir frequently

- At the end of the suggested cooking time remove a noodle and try it. It should be tender, but have a bit of resistance. Because cooking time varies with size and thickness, use the suggested cooking time on the package. With homemade and fresh pasta, the cooking time is considerably shorter than that of dried pasta

- When the noodles are cooked, tip them into a sieve or colander, then immediately into a pre-warmed bowl and coat with sauce so that the pasta doesn't stick together

- The pasta need not be completely drained. Some recipes call for a bit of the cooking water, and moist pasta takes to the sauce better

- When cold pasta is called for, such as in a salad, do not simply let it cool in a colander. Shock it quickly with cold water, and add a little oil or butter to prevent sticking

# Homemade noodles

Dried pasta is simply and quickly prepared, but if you would like to treat your friends or family to something truly special, try serving fresh, homemade egg noodles, or *pasta fatta a casa*, as the Italians say. It does require quite a bit more effort, of course, especially if you don't own a pasta machine, but you will be rewarded with an unsurpassed culinary experience.

Here is a basic recipe to start with (serves 4):

3 cups/400 g flour
4 eggs
$\frac{1}{2}$ tsp salt
1 tbsp olive oil

Mix the flour and salt and form a well in the center. Beat the eggs with a fork. Work the eggs into the flour, then the oil. Gradually incorporate the flour from around the edges.

Knead the dough vigorously for ten minutes, first with a food processor or dough hook, then by hand. It should appear glossy and supple. If it is too stiff, add a little water; if it is too sticky, add some flour.

Finally, form the dough into a ball, cover it with a cloth and let it rest for 30 minutes.

Dust a cutting board or other flat surface with flour, divide the dough into equal portions. Roll them out thinly and evenly, and cut into the desired shape. Before cooking, lay the noodles out on a floured cloth and let them dry so they will be easier to handle.

This basic dough can be expanded, cut into different forms, or used as lasagna noodles or filled with various mixtures. You can also depart from the normal pale yellow color by making coloured pasta. Simply mix the following ingredients into the basic dough to form other colors.

**...een pasta:**

...andful of washed and finely minced herbs, or a half pound of ...nched, squeezed, and finely chopped spinach.

**...llow pasta:**

...sp saffron threads dissolved in 1 tsp lukewarm water

**...rk red pasta:**

...-3 blanched red beets pressed through a sieve

**...r light red pasta:**

...tbsp tomato paste

**For orange pasta:**

several tbsps cooked, puréed red pepper

**Light brown pasta:**

1 oz/25 g dried porcini mushrooms, rehydrated in 1 tbsp hot water and very finely chopped

**Black pasta:**

1 tsp squid ink

In some cases, the dough may require additional flour so that it does not become too sticky.

11

## pes of pasta

he recipes in this book demonstrate, pasta is amazingly
ed and versatile. The many different types of commercially
ilable pasta are equally varied and versatile. The preference
certain forms of pasta may differ from region to region, but
most important thing is to choose the ideal combination of
ta and sauce.

e firm rule of thumb is the following: the thicker and chunkier
sauce, the wider the pasta should be. Pasta that is twisted
wavy will hold more sauce.

th light sauces, thinner, longer pasta is recommended.
turally, there are exceptions to this rule. There are so many
pes that are appealing to the eye, and experimenting with
rm and colour can be very exciting.

e illustration on the opposite page shows some of the most
miliar and most popular types of pasta.

1. Fusilli
2. Lasagne
3. Linguine
4. Macaroni
5. Orecchiette
6. Pappardelle
7. Penne
8. Penne rigate
9. Ravioli
10. Rigatoni
11. Spaghetti
12. Spaghettini
13. Tagliatelle
14. Tortellini
15. Tortelloni
16. Vermicelli

## The names and their meanings

The names of pastas frequently provides some insight into their
characteristics. Let's look at some of the word endings:

- -ine or -ini means "little," and signifies a thin or fine
  form of pasta, such as spaghettini, tortellini or linguine

- -oni means "large," and indicates a large or thick form
  of pasta, for example, tortelloni, rigatoni or macaroni

- -elle refers to a wide pasta, as in tagliatelle

- -ette also indicates a small pasta, like orecchiette

- *rigate* means ribbed, as in penne rigate

## Abbreviations

| | |
|---|---|
| tbsp | tablespoon |
| tsp | teaspoon |
| in | inch |
| cm | centimeter |
| oz | ounce |
| g | gram |
| lb | pound |
| kg | kilogram |
| ml | milliliter |
| l | liter |
| qt | quart |
| kJ | kiloJoule |
| kcal | kilocalorie |
| °C | degree centigrade |
| °F | degree Fahrenheit |

# Classics

Certain pasta sauces have become perennial favorites around the world. Specialties such as Spaghetti Carbonara, Spaghetti Bolognese or Tortellini Quattro Formaggi are known in every country, and for good reason. In this chapter some of the greatest classics among pasta recipes are presented—favorite dishes for the whole family!

# Spaghetti Carbonara

**Serves 4**

2 slices bacon

3½ oz/100 g cooked ham

1 clove garlic

2 tbsp butter

14 oz/400 g spaghetti

salt

3 eggs

7 tbsp/100 ml cream

6 tbsp/40 g
grated Parmesan

6 tbsp/40 g
grated pecorino cheese

ground pepper

*Prep. time: ca. 20 min.
(plus cooking time)
Per portion ca. 703 kcal/2951 kJ
31 g P, 33 g F, 70 g C*

1   Cut the bacon and ham in small cubes. Mince the garlic. Melt the butter in a frying pan and sauté the bacon. Add the garlic, and sauté about 3 minutes longer.

2   Cook the spaghetti until al dente in ample salted water, then drain. Add the pasta to the pan with the bacon and garlic, and stir well.

3   Whisk the eggs together with the cream and half of each of the cheeses. Season with salt and pepper. Stir in the cubed ham. Add this mixture to the spaghetti and stir well, until the eggs begin to solidify.

4   Toss the rest of the cheese with the spaghetti and serve immediately.

**Serves 4**

1 onion, 1 clove garlic

3 slices bacon

1 carrot

½ rib celery

2 tbsp olive oil

14 oz/400 g ground meat

7 tbsp/100 ml red wine

salt, pepper

7 tbsp/100 ml milk

1 tsp chopped fresh oregano

1 can diced tomatoes
(14½ oz/400 g)

1 tbsp sugar

14 oz/400 g spaghetti

7 tbsp/50 g
grated Parmesan

fresh thyme to garnish

*Prep. time: ca. 30 min.*
*(plus cooking time)*
*Per portion ca. 733 kcal/3079 kJ*
*41 g P, 28 g F, 76 g C*

# Spaghetti Bolognese

1  Peel and chop the onion and garlic. Dice the bacon. Peel the carrot, wash the celery rib and chop both. Render the bacon in hot oil. Brown the vegetables, then the meat, stirring frequently.

2  Pour in the red wine and let mixture cook until the liquid is absorbed. Season with salt and pepper. Stir in the milk and continue cooking until the sauce becomes creamy and thick. Add the oregano, tomatoes, and sugar and simmer over low heat for about 30 minutes.

3  Cook the spaghetti according to package instructions, then drain. Arrange the pasta on plates, top with sauce, and sprinkle grated cheese on top. Garnish with fresh thyme and serve.

# Macaroni with Chanterelle Sauce

Peel and finely chop the onions. Cut the bacon in narrow [strips]. Trim the chanterelles and, if necessary, quickly wash in still [water] (do not soak in water). Halve the larger mushrooms. Cook [the m]acaroni in salted water according to package instructions. [Drain] in a colander or sieve.

Heat the oil in a skillet, and fry the bacon strips until crisp. [Rem]ove them with a slotted spoon. Melt the butter in the bacon [drip]pings. Stir in the onions and chanterelles and sauté until all the [liqui]d has evaporated.

3  Stir the crème fraiche and bacon into the mushrooms and heat through. Season with salt and pepper. Stir in the chives and 1 tbsp of the chopped marjoram leaves. Toss the mixture with the macaroni and top with the remaining marjoram leaves.

## Tip:
Instead of chanterelles, you may substitute champignons, oyster mushrooms, porcini or chestnuts. If you leave out the bacon, you will have a wonderful vegetarian meal.

**Serves 4**
2 onions
4 slices bacon
generous 1 lb/500 g
fresh chanterelles
14 oz/400 g macaroni
salt
2 tbsp oil
1½ tbsp/25 g butter
5 oz/150 g crème fraîche
or sour cream
pepper
1 bunch chives, chopped
2 tbsp chopped
fresh marjoram leaves

*Prep. time: ca. 30 min.*
*Per portion ca. 590 kcal/2478 kJ*
*20 g P, 24 g F, 72 g C*

**19**

# Broad Noodles with Mushrooms

1  Clean and slice the mushrooms. Peel the garlic and onion [a]nd mince them. Bring 3 quarts/3 liters water to a boil in a large [p]ot, add a pinch of salt, and cook the noodles until al dente [a]ccording to the package instructions.

2  In a large pan melt the butter and sweat the onions. Add [t]he garlic, then the mushrooms, and sauté on medium heat for [a]bout 5 minutes. Season with the paprika. Pour on the vegetable [b]roth and cook over high heat until the liquid is reduced by half. [S]tir in the sour cream and season with salt, pepper, and the [l]emon juice.

3  Rinse, dry and chop the parsley finely. Stir half of it into the sauce. Drain the noodles and divide them among preheated plates. Pour the sauce over the noodles and sprinkle with the rest of the parsley. Serve while hot.

**Serves 4**
generous 1 lb/500 g
champignons
2 cloves garlic
1 onion
salt
14 oz/400 g wide noodles
2 tbsp butter
2 tbsp sharp paprika
1 cup/250 ml
vegetable broth
½ cup/125 g sour cream
pepper
2 tbsp lemon juice
1 bunch parsley

*Prep. time: ca. 30 min.*
*Per portion ca. 475 kcal/1995 kJ*
*17 g P, 13 g F, 71 g C*

# Spaghetti Aglio e Olio

**Serves 4**

14 oz/400 g spaghetti

salt

**5 cloves garlic**

**1 bunch flat-leaf parsley**

**½ fresh red chilli pepper**

**¼ cup/60 ml**
**extra virgin olive oil**

**1 dried chili pepper**

**pepper**

*Prep. time: ca. 20 min.*
*Per portion ca. 493 kcal/2070 kJ*
*13 g P, 18 g F, 70 g C*

1   Cook the spaghetti according to package instructions.

2   Peel and thinly slice the garlic. Rinse, dry and finely chop the parsley, setting aside 1 tbsp. Wash and deseed the red pepper, then chop it or slice into thin strips.

3   Slowly heat the oil in a pan and sauté the red pepper for 2 minutes. Add the garlic and sauté briefly, but do not let it brown or it will become bitter. Crumble the dried chili pepper into the pan.

4   Drain the spaghetti and add it to the other ingredients with the chopped parsley. Mix well, season with salt and pepper, and garnish with the remaining parsley.

# Pasta with Parmesan & Brown Butter

1   Warm the plates. Cook the noodles in boiling salted water according to the package instructions.

2   Lightly brown the butter in a frying pan.

3   Drain the noodles and toss with the butter. Immediately distribute on the warmed plates and sprinkle with the cheese.

**Serves 4**

**14 oz/400 g wide noodles**

**salt**

**⅔ cup/150 g butter**

**scant 1 cup/100 g**
**freshly grated Parmesan**

*Prep. time: ca. 20 min.*
*Per portion ca. 828 kcal/3466 kJ*
*24 g P, 43 g F, 86 g C*

20

**Serves 4**

14 oz/400 g spaghetti

salt

1 onion

1 tbsp butter or margarine

1 tbsp flour

generous 1½ cups/375 ml milk, heated

7 tbsp/50 g each: grated Gruyère, Gouda, and Parmesan cheeses

freshly ground pepper

freshly ground nutmeg

⅓ cup/50 g pine nuts

1 tbsp chopped fresh thyme

*Prep. time: ca. 30 min.*
*Per portion ca. 695 kcal/2913 kJ*
*30 g P, 30 g F, 77 g C*

# Spaghetti with Cheese Sauce

1 Cook the spaghetti in salted water according to package instructions, then drain.

2 Peel and finely chop the onion. Melt the butter in a large saucepan, add the onion, and sweat until transparent. Dust with the flour, stir, and cook until golden. Pour in the warm milk and mix well. Simmer on low heat for 5 minutes, stirring frequently.

3 Add the grated Gruyere, Gouda, and most of the Parmesan. Continue to stir on low heat until the cheeses have melted. Season well with salt, pepper, and nutmeg.

4 Lightly toast pine nuts in a pan with no fat. Toss the spaghetti with the cheese sauce. Sprinkle with the pine nuts, remaining Parmesan, and fresh thyme.

# Macaroni in Gorgonzola Sauce

Remove any rind from the Gorgonzola, cut it in cubes and melt in a large saucepan on low heat. When the cheese has melted, stir in the cream and season to taste with salt, pepper and a pinch of sugar. Allow the sauce to thicken, stirring constantly, 3–5 minutes.

$2$  Cut the ham slices in half and add to the cheese sauce to warm through. Cook the macaroni according to the package instructions. Pour the cheese sauce over the cooked, drained macaroni, sprinkle with finely chopped parsley, and serve.

**Serves 4**
5 oz/150 g Gorgonzola
1 cup/250 ml cream
salt
pepper
sugar
5 oz/150 g prosciutto
(6–8 slices)
14 oz/400 g macaroni
fresh parsley, minced

*Prep. time: ca. 25 min.*
*Per portion ca. 905 kcal/3801 kJ*
*35 g P, 46 g F, 87 g C*

23

**Serves 4**

1 bunch watercress

5 tbsp/40 g pine nuts

7 tbsp/50 g freshly
grated Parmesan

pepper

8 tbsp olive oil

14 oz/400 g spaghetti

salt

*Prep. time: ca. 35 min.*
*Per portion ca. 659 kcal/2755 kJ*
*21 g P, 31 g F, 69 g C*

## Spaghetti with Watercress Pesto

1 Wash and dry the cress. Pluck the leaves off the stems and mince with the pine nuts. Combine the cress mixture with half of the grated Parmesan and some pepper. Add the oil and stir until the mixture has thickened.

2 Cook the spaghetti according to package instructions, then drain. Portion out the pasta on plates and place a generous tbsp of pesto on each portion. Sprinkle with the remaining Parmesan and serve.

**Serves 4**

1 bunch parsley

1 bunch fresh basil

2 cloves garlic

7 tbsp/50 g
chopped almonds

2 tbsp grated pecorino

2 tbsp olive oil

½ dried chili

½ cup/125 ml bouillon

salt

14 oz/400 g tagliatelle

*Prep. time: ca. 30 min.*
*Per portion ca. 458 kcal/1924 kJ*
*16 g P, 12 g F, 70 g C*

## Tagliatelle with Parsley-Almond Pesto

1 Wash, dry, pluck and finely chop the parsley and basil leaves (you should have about 1 cup of each). Mix the herbs, peeled garlic cloves and almonds in a food processor or blender. Add the cheese, oil and crushed chili. Pulse to blend. Add the bouillon and season to taste.

2 Cook the pasta in salted water according to package instructions. Drain, reserving about ½ cup/120 ml of the cooking water. Toss the pasta with the pesto, adding a little cooking water as needed.

**Serves 4**

3½ oz/100 g
sun-dried tomatoes

⅓ cup/50 g almonds

7 tbsp/60 g pine nuts

¾ cup/80 g
grated Parmesan

½ bunch fresh parsley

1 bunch fresh basil

1–2 tbsp balsamic vinegar

1 pinch sugar

pepper

14 oz/400 g spaghetti

*Prep. time: ca. 25 min.*
*Per portion ca. 605 kcal/2541 kJ*
*25 g P, 24 g F, 70 g C*

## Spaghetti with Tomato Pesto

1 Cook the tomatoes in boiling salted water for about 5 minutes. Remove the tomatoes, drain, and reserve about ⅔ cup/150 ml of the liquid. Toast the almonds and pine nuts in a dry pan until golden brown. Puree the nuts, tomatoes and Parmesan in a blender or food processor, slowly adding the reserved tomato liquid.

2 Rinse, dry, and mince the parsley and basil. Add them to the purée and blend. Season with the balsamic vinegar, a pinch of sugar, and salt and pepper to taste.

3 Cook the spaghetti al dente. Drain, shock in cold water, and drain again. Mix the pasta with pesto, arrange on plates and serve.

# paghetti with Pesto

Toast the pine nuts in a dry pan. Pluck the basil leaves from stems, then rinse and dry. Peel the garlic. Coarsely chop all ~~e~~ ingredients.

Work the basil, garlic, pine nuts and a little salt to a paste ~~a~~ food processor or blender. Mix in the Parmesan and olive oil, ~~d~~ season with pepper.

3 Cook the spaghetti in ample salted water until al dente, according to the package instructions. Toss with the pesto and serve immediately.

**Serves 4**

**1 tbsp pine nuts**

**1½ bunches fresh basil**

**1 clove garlic**

**salt**

**3 tbsp grated Parmesan**

**¼ cup/60 ml olive oil**

**pepper**

**generous 1 lb/500 g spaghetti**

*Prep. time: ca. 30 min.*
*Per portion ca. 518 kcal/2176 kJ*
*17 g P, 11 g F, 86 g C*

25

# Fettuccine with Lemon Sauce

Rinse the lemon in hot water. Peel the lemon rind with a [lem]on zester, or peel with a knife, and cut the zest into thin strips. [Sq]ueeze out the lemon juice.

2 Wash and dry the sage leaves and cut them into fine strips. [He]at the oil and fry the sage for 2–3 minutes, then remove with [a s]lotted spoon. Add the flour to the hot oil, then stir in 4 tbsp [lem]on juice, half the lemon peel, the milk and the stock. Simmer [for] 10 minutes, stirring constantly, then remove from the heat.

3 Cook the noodles in boiling salted water according to package instructions. Beat the egg yolks and cream together. Stir 3 tbsp of the hot lemon sauce into the yolk mixture, then stir this mixture and the rest of the egg yolks into the hot sauce. Season with salt and pepper.

4 Drain the noodles and pour over the sauce. Serve garnished with lemon slices, sage strips, and sage leaves.

**Serves 4**
1 untreated lemon
4–6 sage leaves
6 tbsp olive oil
2 tbsp flour
1 cup/250 ml milk
1 cup/250 ml vegetable stock
14 oz/400 g fettuccine
salt
½ cup/125 ml cream
2 egg yolks
pepper
lemon slices to garnish
sage leaves to garnish

*Prep. time: ca. 25 min.*
*Per portion ca. 696 kcal/2909 kJ*
*18 g P, 33 g F, 76 g C*

27

# Spaghettini with Spinach

1 Cull, wash, and dry the spinach. Rinse the chili peppers, [h]alve and deseed them, and dice the pods. Peel and finely chop the garlic.

2 Cook the spaghettini until al dente in ample salted water, according to the package instructions.

3 Heat the oil in a frying pan and sauté the chilis. Add the garlic and cook, stirring constantly, until transparent. Stir in the sesame seeds and brown them for about 2 minutes, continuing to stir. Add the spinach and let it wilt.

4 Drain the pasta, shock with cold running water, and drain it again.

5 Season the spinach mixture to taste with salt and pepper. Arrange in pasta dishes and serve.

**Serves 4**
11 oz/300 g fresh spinach
3 red chili peppers
4 cloves garlic
14 oz/400 g spaghettini
salt
⅔ cup/150 ml olive oil
6 tbsp/50 g sesame seeds
pepper

*Prep. time: ca. 25 min.*
*Per portion ca. 373 kcal/1564 kJ*
*14 g P, 3 g F, 70 g C*

**Serves 4**

scant 3 cups/400 g flour

5 eggs

salt

14 oz/400 g mushrooms

1 clove garlic

1 onion

1 bunch flat-leaf parsley

½ bunch fresh thyme

2½ tbsp/40 g butter

7 tbsp/100 ml white wine

pepper

6 tbsp/100 g ricotta

6 tbsp/40 g freshly
grated Parmesan

11 oz/300 g tomatoes

4 tbsp olive oil

2 tbsp chopped chives

*Prep. time: ca. 35 min.
(plus resting and cooking time)
Per portion ca. 714 kcal/2999 kJ
26 g P, 30 g F, 77 g C*

# Ravioli

1    On a flat work surface, sift the flour into a mound and form a well in the middle. Tip 4 eggs and a little salt in the well. Work by hand into a smooth dough, adding 1–2 tbsp water. If needed, add some additional flour. Knead the dough with dough hooks if using a standing mixer, or in a food processor, for about 5 minutes, until it is firm and elastic. Wrap the dough in plastic wrap and chill in the refrigerator for 30 minutes.

2    Wash and finely chop the mushrooms. Peel and mince the garlic and onion. Rinse, shake dry and finely mince the parsley and thyme leaves. Heat half of the butter in a frying pan, add half the mushrooms, and sauté for 3 minutes. Add half of the onion and garlic, and sauté 2–3 minutes longer. Pour on half the wine and scrape the pan. Add half the herbs and cook 3 minutes longer, season with salt and pepper, and allow to cool. Repeat the process with the remaining ingredients. Separate the remaining egg. Add the egg yolk, ricotta, and half of the Parmesan to the cooled mushroom mixture and blend.

3    Divide the dough in two. On a floured surface, roll out to rectangles about ⅛ inch thick. Cut the dough into long strips 4 in/10 cm wide. On two of the strips, place spoonfuls of filling at intervals of 1–1½ in/3–4 cm, leaving about ½ in/1 cm at the outer edges of each dollop. Whisk the egg white with 2 tbsp water and use a pastry brush to brush it on the pasta not covered by filling. Top with two strips of dough, press lightly around the filling, and cut the ravioli apart with a pastry wheel or a glass. Lay them on a floured board.

4    Slide the ravioli into a generous quantity of salted boiling water, cook 6–8 minutes or until al dente, drain, and shock with cold water. Score the skin of the tomatoes, scald with boiling water, peel, deseed, and cut into large cubes. Heat the olive oil and sauté the ravioli briefly. Add the tomatoes, sauté an additional minute, then add salt and pepper. Sprinkle with the remaining Parmesan cheese and the chives and serve.

# Spaghetti al Pomodoro

**Serves 4**

14 oz/400 g spaghetti

salt

2–3 lb/1–1.5 kg
ripe plum tomatoes

2 shallots

1 small piece chili
pepper

6 tbsp olive oil

12 fresh basil leaves

7 oz/200 g mozzarella

*Prep. time: ca. 30 min.*
*Per portion ca. 553 kcal/2323 kJ*
*25 g P, 16 g F, 76  g C*

1 Cook the spaghetti in ample salted water until al dente, according to the package instructions. Score the skin of the tomatoes, remove the stem, scald with boiling water, and peel. Remove the seeds and dice the flesh.

2 Peel and chop shallots. Remove the seeds from the chili and cut in small strips. Mix all of these together, season with salt and pepper, and stir in the olive oil. Wash, dry and cut the basil leaves in strips. Blend everything with the tomatoes.

3 Cut the mozzarella in ¾ in/2 cm cubes. Drain the spaghetti well, then tip it into a large pot and add the tomatoes and cheese. Stir over low heat for a few minutes until the mozzarella begins to melt.

# Spaghetti with Peppers, Tomatoes & Gorgonzola

1 Bring salted water to the boil for the spaghetti. If using fresh tomatoes, score the skin, scald with boiling water, peel, remove the seeds and chop. Deseed the peppers and cut in strips.

2 Heat the olive oil in a large skillet and briefly sauté the garlic. Add the pepper strips and sauté for 5 minutes, stirring constantly. Sprinkle on salt. Cook the spaghetti in ample salted water until al dente, according to the package instructions.

3 Add the diced tomatoes to the pan and season with the oregano and chili powder. Cook the sauce for 8–10 minutes, stirring occasionally, and season with salt. Trim, rinse and slice the scallion.

4 Tip the drained spaghetti into a prewarmed bowl and mix with the crumbled Gorgonzola. Add the pepper tomato sauce, toss well and garnish with scallion. Sprinkle with Parmesan cheese before serving.

**Serves 4**

**14 oz/400 g spaghetti**

**generous 1 lb/500 g fresh tomatoes or 1 14½-oz can peeled tomatoes**

**3 yellow peppers**

**2 tbsp olive oil**

**4 cloves garlic, minced**

**1 pinch oregano**

**1 pinch chili powder**

**5 oz/150 g Gorgonzola**

**1 scallion**

**¾ cup/80 g freshly grated Parmesan**

*Prep. time: ca. 30 min.*
*Per portion ca. 643 kcal/2701 kJ*
*29 g P, 25 g F, 75 g C*

# Macaroni al Carciofi

1  Cut the stems from the artichokes and remove the small ...gh leaves. Cut the points from the outer leaves with scissors, ... cut the point out of the top with a knife. Remove the choke ... immediately place the artichokes in cold water with 1 tbsp ...on juice. When all the artichokes are ready to cook, remove ...m from the lemon water and drain. Place them in a large pot ... water. Add the remaining the lemon juice and some salt. ...g to the boil, cover the pot, and cook for about 15 minutes. ...e they are cooked, cut in quarters.

2  Wash the tomatoes, score the skin, remove the stems, scald ...h boiling water, and peel. Remove the seeds and dice.

3  Peel and finely dice the onion, garlic, and carrots. Wash and dry the celery stalk and mince it as well.

4  Heat the olive oil in a skillet and sauté the vegetables for 3–5 minutes. Add the chopped tomatoes and stock, and season with salt and pepper. Simmer, covered, for 10 minutes.

5  Cook the macaroni until al dente in ample salted water. Drain, shock with cold water, and drain again. Serve the pasta with the artichokes and sauce, garnished with fresh thyme.

**Serves 4**

12 small artichokes
2 tbsp lemon juice
salt
1¼ lb/600 g tomatoes
3 onions
1 clove garlic
2 carrots
2 ribs celery
2 tbsp olive oil
½ cup/125 ml
vegetable stock
pepper
14 oz/400 g macaroni
thyme to garnish

*Prep. time: ca. 30 min.*
*(plus cooking and baking time)*
*Per portion ca. 393 kcal/1649 kJ*
*9 g P, 4 g F, 68 g C*

**33**

# Penne all'Arrabbiata

1  Cook the pasta in ample salted water until al dente, according to the package instructions. Add the peas (thawed) to the cooking water 2 minutes before the noodles are ready.

2  Purée the tomato paste, ketchup, garlic, capers, and olive oil together. Season with salt and a pinch of sugar. Remove the seeds from the chili, mince, and mix with the pesto.

3  Rinse, dry and finely chop the parsley. Drain the pasta and peas and combine with the pesto, chopped parsley, and black olives. Sprinkle with Parmesan and serve.

**Serves 4**

14 oz/400 g penne
salt
11 oz/300 g frozen peas
1 bunch parsley, chopped
2 tbsp tomato paste
1 tbsp ketchup
1 clove garlic
1–2 tsp capers
2 tbsp olive oil
sugar, 1 red chili
3 oz/80 g black olives
6 tbsp/40 g
grated Parmesan

*Prep. time: ca. 20 min.*
*Per portion ca. 510 kcal/2142 kJ*
*22 g P, 15 g F, 83 g C*

**Serves 4**

generous 2 cups/300 g
flour

salt

5 eggs

2 oz/50 g turkey or
chicken breast

3½ oz/100 g pork cutlet

1 tbsp butter

3½ oz/100 g prosciutto

3½ oz/100 g mortadella

1¾ cups/200 g
grated Parmesan

pepper

nutmeg

2 qt/2 l chicken or
beef stock

*Prep. time: ca. 30 min.
(plus resting and cooking time)
Per portion ca. 738 kcal/3100 kJ
54 g P, 34 g F, 54 g C*

**34**

# Tortellini with Meat Filling

1 Prepare a pasta dough from the flour, a pinch of salt, and 3 eggs. Cover with a damp cloth and let it rest for 30 minutes.

2 For the filling, cut the poultry breast and pork in small cubes and brown in the butter (about 10 minutes). Allow to cool, then blend in a food processor with the ham and mortadella. Work the meats into a paste with the remaining 2 eggs, 1⅓ cups/150 g of the Parmesan, salt, freshly ground pepper, and nutmeg. Refrigerate the filling for several hours, or if possible, overnight.

3 Use a rolling pin to roll out the dough to the thickness of a knife blade. Cut out circles with a small glass or biscuit cutter (1½ in/4 cm diameter) or cut into squares. Place a nut-sized dollop of filling in the middle of each and press together in a half moon or triangle. Press the edges tightly together. Wrap around an index finger and press both ends together to form a ring shape.

4 Bring the stock to a boil in a wide, deep stock pot, adding salt if desired, and add the tortellini to the pot in portions. Cook each batch about 5 minutes. Serve in the broth, sprinkled with the remaining Parmesan cheese.

# ortellini Quattro Formaggi

Cook the pasta until al dente in salted water according to package instructions, then drain. Peel and mince the onion. e and dry the sage leaves and cut into fine strips. Cut the ses in cubes.

Melt 1 tbsp of the butter in a large saucepan and sauté the on until transparent. Pour in the cream. Add the cheese cubes I melt over low heat, stirring constantly. Season the cheese ce with salt and pepper.

3 Wash, dry and halve the tomatoes. Melt the rest of the butter in a frying pan. Add the tomatoes and sage strips, briefly sauté, and again season with salt and pepper.

4 Arrange the pasta on prewarmed plates, top with the sauce and tomatoes, and serve.

**Serves 4**
¾ lb/350 g tortellini
**salt**
**1 onion**
**4 sage leaves**
**2 oz/50 g each:**
**mozzarella, Gorgonzola,**
**brie, and Gouda cheeses**
**2 tbsp butter**
**7 tbsp/100 ml cream**
**pepper**
**5 oz/150 g**
**cherry tomatoes**

*Prep. time: ca. 30 min.*
*Per portion ca. 320 kcal/1344 kJ*
*15 g P, 25 g F, 9 g C*

35

# Pasta & Seafood

Between the Riviera and the Adriatic and Aegean Seas, Italy is surrounded by water. It is no wonder, then, that Italian cuisine has incorporated freshly caught fish and seafood and melded it with every conceivable variation of pasta, as well. Whether shrimp, mussels, swordfish or sardines, these recipes demonstrate the imaginative and delicious dishes that can be created with the bounty of the sea.

# Penne with Crayfish

**Serves 4**

24 frozen crayfish

2 shallots

2½ tbsp/35 g butter

1 tbsp curry powder

1 tbsp honey

⅔ cup/150 ml white wine

14 oz/400 g peeled
tomatoes (canned)

2 cups/500 ml
whipping cream

salt, cayenne pepper

⅓ cup/40 g raisins

½ cup/70 g pine nuts

1 tbsp olive oil

14 oz/400 g penne

1 small bunch basil

*Prep. time: ca. 40 min.
(plus cooking time)
Per portion ca. 1151 kcal/4815 kJ
35 g P, 62 g F, 105 g C*

1  Let crayfish thaw. Remove the tails from the bodies with a light twist. Break open the tail shells, make an incision in the meat along the back, remove the innards, and chill.

2  Peel and dice the shallots. Brown them in butter along with the crayfish bodies and shells over high heat. Quickly stir in the curry powder, then add the honey, 7 tbsp/100 ml of the white wine, and the tomatoes with their juice. Reduce this for 5 minutes. Stir in the cream, and season with salt and cayenne pepper. Let the sauce simmer over medium heat for 10 minutes.

3  Boil the raisins in the remaining white wine until all the liquid has evaporated. Sauté the pine nuts in the olive oil, turni them frequently, until they are golden brown. Cook the penne in ample salted water until al dente according to the package instructions, then drain.

4  Pour the sauce through a fine sieve, pressing the last of i through. Blend the raisins, crayfish tails and penne into the sauc and heat. Serve sprinkled with a few fresh basil leaves and the pine nuts.

**Serves 4**

14 oz/400 g shrimp,
ready to eat

2½ tbsp/40 g crab paste

1 onion

1 tbsp flour

1 cup/250 ml
whipping cream

1 cup/250 ml white wine

14 oz/400 g pasta shells

1 bunch fresh dill

1 tbsp fine orange zest

½ cup/125 ml orange juice

salt

pepper

*Prep. time: ca. 30 min.*
*Per portion ca. 718 kcal/3004 kJ*
*34 g P, 31 g F, 69 g C*

# Shells with Shrimp in Orange Sauce

1  Rinse the shrimp and dab dry. Heat the crab paste in a pan and brown the shrimp for about 1 minute on each side, then remove from the pan with a slotted spoon.

2  Peel and dice the onions, then add to the same pan and sweat. Sprinkle the flour over them, stir, and brown lightly. Pour in the cream and wine. Reduce the heat to low and let the sauce simmer for 10 minutes. In the meantime, cook the pasta until al dente, according to the package instructions.

3  Add the shrimp to the sauce and heat 2 minutes. Rinse and shake dry the dill, setting aside a few sprigs for garnish, then chop the rest. Add the chopped dill, orange zest, and orange juice to sauce. Season with salt and pepper.

4  Drain the pasta shells. Serve with orange sauce and garnished with the remaining dill.

# Penne with Scampi

Wash the scampi or shrimp thoroughly. Carefully peel from shell and remove the innards. Wash the vegetables and cut in into small pieces. In a pot combine the empty shells with the vegetables, peppercorns, and a pinch of salt. Add enough water to cover everything, bring to a boil, and simmer for 15 minutes. Pour the broth through a fine sieve.

Bring the broth back to a boil and steep the mullet fillet and parsley in it for 3 minutes. Remove the parsley and chop it for later use. Pureé the broth and fish in a blender. Cut the scampi in pieces.

Heat the olive oil in a large pan. Peel and mince the garlic, then sauté it until golden. Add the scampi and chopped parsley and briefly sauté. Season with salt and pepper to taste.

4 Cook the pasta in ample salted water until al dente, according to the package instructions. Drain the pasta, reserving some of the cooking water.

5 Add the penne to the pan with the scampi. Add the fish pureé, and if necessary, thin it a little with some of the pasta cooking water. Combine everything thoroughly over low heat. Finally, blend the finely chopped sorrel and thin slices of butter into the pasta dish. Serve immediately on warm plates.

**Serves 4**

16 fresh scampi or shrimp in the shell

10 peppercorns

1 carrot

1 rib celery

1 small onion

salt

3½ oz/100 g mullet fillet

2 stalks fresh parsley

5 tbsp olive oil

1 clove garlic

2 tbsp chopped parsley

white pepper

14 oz/400 g penne

2 large sorrel leaves

2 tbsp/30 g butter

*Prep. time: ca. 40 min.*
*Per portion ca. 565 kcal/2373 kJ*
*29 g P, 17 g F, 72 g C*

**41**

# Spaghetti with Shrimp & Yellow Peppers

1 Wash and dry the shrimp. Peel and dice the onion. Clean the yellow pepper and slice in thin strips. Heat 3 tbsp of the olive oil and sauté the onions until translucent, then add the peppers. Salt lightly and sweat over low heat until tender.

2 Cook the spaghetti in ample salted water until al dente, according to the package instructions. Drain the pasta, retaining some of the cooking water.

3 Heat the remaining oil in a large pan, briefly brown the shrimp, then pour in the wine and add salt. Bring to a boil and cook over high heat for about 3 minutes. Add the tender pepper strips and continue to boil briefly.

4 Add the cooked spaghetti to the shrimp in the pan. Over low heat, add the parsley and gently blend together all the ingredients. Sprinkle with freshly ground pepper before serving.

**Serves 4**

9 oz/250 g shrimp, ready to eat

1 small onion

½ yellow pepper

6 tbsp olive oil

salt

14 oz/400 g spaghetti

3½ tbsp/50 ml white wine

1 tbsp chopped parsley

white pepper

*Prep. time: ca. 40 min.*
*Per portion ca. 503 kcal/2113 kJ*
*26 g P, 11 g F, 71 g C*

# Rigatoni with Swordfish

**Serves 4**

4 tbsp olive oil

1 clove garlic

14 oz/400 g ripe tomatoes

7 tbsp/100 ml white wine

1 chili pepper

6 fresh mint leaves

11 oz/300 g swordfish

14 oz/400 g rigatoni

generous ½ cup/60 g
freshly grated Parmesan

mint leaves to garnish

*Prep. time: ca. 30 min.
(plus cooking time)
Per portion ca. 588 kcal/2470 kJ
33 g P, 16 g F, 72 g C*

1   Heat the olive oil in a pan. Peel the garlic and sauté until golden brown.

2   Score the tomatoes across the top, remove the stalks, scald in boiling water, skin, and remove the seeds. Dice the tomato flesh and add it to pan. Pour in the wine and bring to a boil.

3   Wash and dry the chili and mint leaves, cut into very fine slices, and add to the tomatoes. Rinse and pat dry the fish, slice it thinly, and add to the pan as well. Stew everything over low heat for approximately 10 minutes.

4   Cook the rigatoni in ample salted water until al dente, according to the package instructions. Drain the pasta, then add it to the pan with the fish. Carefully stir all ingredients together for 1 minute over low heat. Serve on warmed plates, garnished with freshly grated Parmesan and fresh mint leaves.

# Penne with Tuna & Tomato Sauce

**Serves 4**

14 oz/400 g penne

2 onions

1–2 cloves garlic

2–3 dried chili peppers

3 tbsp oil

1 large can (ca. 26 oz)
peeled tomatoes

2 oz/50 g black olives

⅓ cup/50 g capers

1 tbsp sugar

salt

pepper

1 bunch flat-leaf parsley

2 cans tuna fish

*Prep. time: ca. 30 min.
Per portion ca. 739 kcal /3090 kJ
36 g P, 28 g F, 80 g C*

1   Cook the penne in salted water according to package instructions.

2   Peel and mince the onions and garlic. Finely chop the chili peppers. Heat the oil and sauté the onions until translucent. Add the garlic and chili peppers and continue to cook.

3   Add tomatoes with their liquid and let simmer, uncovered, for about 10 minutes. Remove the pits from the olives, drain the capers, and add both to the sauce. Season with the sugar and salt and pepper to taste.

4   Rinse, dry, and finely chop the parsley. Drain the tuna fish and use a fork to break it up into pieces. Before serving, mix the parsley and tuna into the sauce and serve with the penne.

# Penne with Yellow Pepper, Capers & Anchovies

**Serves 4**

**3–4 yellow bell peppers**

**2 cloves garlic**

**6 tbsp olive oil**

**12 anchovies in water**

**14 oz/400 g penne**

**2 tbsp capers**

**fresh basil and**
**mint leaves**

**salt**

**pepper**

*Prep. time: ca. 30 min.*
*Per portion ca. 450 kcal/1890 kJ*
*18 g P, 19 g F, 73 g C*

1  Cut the peppers in half, wash them, then broil in the oven until the skin blisters and peels. Peel the peppers, then cut into thin strips. Finely mince the garlic.

2  Heat half of the olive oil in a pan and fry the garlic, chopped anchovies and the pepper strips over low heat. Cook the penne to al dente in salted water, according to the package instructions.

3  Add the capers to the peppers and anchovies and stew together for a few minutes. Add the finely chopped basil and mint leaves, then season with salt to taste. When the pasta is ready, pour off the water and allow to drain. Tip the pasta into the pan with the peppers.

4  Stir in the remaining oil. Blend everything well and heat through over low heat for another 1–2 minutes. Serve sprinkled with freshly ground pepper.

# ¡paghetti with Pesto & Fillet of Fish

Combine the pine nuts, 7 tbsp/100 ml of the olive oil, the
[garli]c and basil leaves and puree in a blender. Blend the Parmesan
[into] the pesto and season with salt and pepper to taste.

Cook the spaghetti until al dente according to the package
[inst]ructions. Then drain, rinse under cold water, drain thoroughly,
[and] toss in 1 tbsp olive oil.

3 Score the tomatoes across the top, blanch in boiling water,
remove the skin and seeds, and dice the flesh. Season the fish
with salt and pepper, and in the remaining olive oil, fry it on both
sides until golden brown.

4 Heat the spaghetti, toss it thoroughly with the pesto, and
distribute among the plates. Sprinkle each portion with diced
tomatoes and top with a fried fish fillet. Garnish with fresh basil.

**Serves 4**

**⅔ cup/100 g pine nuts**

**9 tbsp/130 ml olive oil**

**3 cloves garlic, peeled**

**1¾ oz/50 g basil leaves**

**7 tbsp/50 g**
**grated Parmesan**

**14 oz/400 g spaghetti**

**9 oz/250 g tomatoes**

**14 oz/400 g fillet of bass,**
**halibut or flounder**

**salt**

**pepper**

*Prep. time: ca. 25 min.*
*(plus cooking time)*
*Per portion ca. 859 kcal/3590 kJ*
*49 g P, 47 g F, 74 g C*

45

# Black Tagliatelli with Squid

**Serves 4**

14 oz/400 g squid,
fresh or frozen

3 large yellow bell peppers

7 oz/200 g tomatoes

1–2 sprigs basil

2 cloves garlic

9 oz/250 g black tagliatelli

4 tbsp olive oil

2 bay leaves

salt

pepper

1–2 tbsp lemon juice

*Prep. time: ca. 40 min.
(plus resting and cooking time)
Per portion ca. 383 kcal/1609 kJ
26 g P, 8 g F, 51 g C*

1 Allow frozen squid to thaw. Preheat the oven to 480 °F/ 250 °C. Cut the peppers into quarters, then rinse, dry and deseed them. Place the peppers on a baking sheet with the cut sides down. Bake in the oven for 10–15 minutes, or until the skin forms dark blisters. Place the peppers in a freezer bag and set them aside for 15 minutes.

2 Peel the skin from the peppers, then cut them in strips. Score the tops of the tomatoes, remove the stalks, blanch in boiling water, then skin and remove the seeds. Dice the tomato flesh. Wash the basil, shake it dry, then pluck the leaves and chop them coarsely. Peel and mince the garlic. Rinse the squid, dab dry, and cut into pieces.

3 Cook the pasta until al dente, according to the package instructions. Pour off the cooking water and drain the pasta. Heat 2 tbsp of the olive oil in a large pan. Add the squid, garlic, and bay leaves. Fry over high heat, stirring frequently, for about 5 minutes.

4 Add the tomatoes and pepper slices to the pan and briefly braise everything together. Season the squid with salt, pepper and the lemon juice. Remove the bay leaves. Combine the squid and pepper mixture with the pasta, remaining olive oil and basil, then serve while hot.

# Sepia Pasta with Seafood

**Serves 4**

11 oz/300 g seafood,
fresh or frozen

2 carrots, 1 leek

½ celery rib

2 tbsp butter

7 tbsp/100 ml
lobster stock

½ cup/125 ml white wine

14 oz/400 g sepia pasta

salt

4–5 oz/125 g
crème fraîche

1 bunch chives

*Prep. time: ca. 35 min.
(plus resting time)
Per portion ca. 540 kcal/2268 kJ
21 g P, 20 g F, 63 g C*

1 Allow frozen seafood to thaw according to package instructions, or clean and prepare fresh seafood. Peel the carrots and cut into thin batons. Trim and wash the leek, then cut into thin rings. Brush and wash the celery rib, dry, and chop into thin pieces.

2 Sauté the vegetables in the butter for about 5–8 minutes. Pour on the lobster broth and white wine, then add the seafood. Cover the pan and braise everything together for 10 minutes.

3 Cook the pasta in ample salted water until al dente, according to the package instructions. Drain and rinse with cold water. Stir the crème fraîche into the seafood-vegetable mix and season to taste with salt.

4 Wash and dry the chives and cut them into little rings. Arrange the pasta and sauce on plates, sprinkle with chopped chives, and serve.

# Turbot on Black Noodles

1   Combine all the ingredients for the dough in a bowl and work them together into a firm yet elastic dough. Set it aside and let it rest for several hours. Use a pasta machine (setting 6) to roll out and cut the pasta dough. Cook the black noodles in ample salted water until al dente, drain, and let cool.

2   For the sauce, bring to a boil the vermouth, white wine, and fish stock with the saffron threads and red pepper. Pour it through a sieve into a second pan. Do not discard the contents of the sieve.

3   Bring the strained sauce to a boil, then turn down the heat and add the cream. Cut the chilled butter into small pieces and gradually blend it into the sauce. Season to taste with the curry, pastis and salt.

4   Season the turbot fillets and poach them in the fish stock for about 5–7 minutes.

5   Pluck the tarragon leaves from the stems and finely chop. Bring the sauce just to a boil and add the rest of the reduction from the sieve, the tarragon and chives, and season.

6   Toss the black noodles in the hot butter and arrange in the center of warm serving plates. Top with a turbot fillet. Pour the sauce around the noodles and over the fish, and serve.

**Serves 4**

**For the pasta dough:**
2¾ cups/400 g flour
4 egg yolks
1 egg
1 tbsp olive oil
7 tbsp/100 ml squid ink
salt

**For the sauce:**
3½ tbsp/50 ml vermouth
3½ tbsp/50 ml white wine
½ cup/120 ml fish stock
a few saffron threads
1 tsp red pepper
¼ cup/60 ml cream
14 tbsp/200 g butter
1 tsp curry
4 tsp/20 ml pastis
(anise liqueur)
salt

4 turbot fillets
generous ¾ cup/200 ml
fish stock
½ bunch tarragon
1 tsp chopped fresh chives
2 tbsp butter

*Prep. time: ca. 35 min.*
*(plus resting and cooking time)*
*Per portion ca. 853 kcal/3583 kJ*
*45 g P, 40 g F, 73 g C*

# Penne with Anchovies

**Serves 4**

14 oz/400 g penne

salt

1 onion

2 cloves garlic

6 anchovy fillets

2 tbsp olive oil

1 can peeled tomatoes

pepper

½ bunch parsley

3½ oz/100 g black olives, pitted

scant 1 cup/100 g grated or shaved pecorino cheese

basil leaves to garnish

*Prep. time: ca. 30 min.*
*Per portion ca. 750 kcal/3150 kJ*
*53 g P, 19 g F, 88 g C*

1 Cook the pasta in ample salted water until al dente, according to the package instructions.

2 Peel and dice the onion and garlic. Cut the anchovy fillets into small pieces. Heat the olive oil and sweat the diced onion and garlic for 3–5 minutes.

3 Add the anchovies and tomatoes to the pan, including their juices. Season everything with salt and pepper. Simmer over medium heat for about 8 minutes, letting the sauce thicken slightly and crushing the tomatoes with a spoon. Wash, shake dry, and finely chop the parsley.

4 Slice the olives. Stir them into the sauce and heat throug then blend in the parsley.

5 Serve the pasta and sauce with a generous topping of shaved or grated pecorino and garnished with fresh basil leaves.

# Spinach Noodles with Scallops

1 Peel and chop the shallot. Wash, shake dry, and finely chop the herbs. In a saucepan, combine the wine and 1 cup/250 ml water with the shallots and all the herbs and spices. Bring to a boil and simmer for about 10 minutes. Put the scallops in the broth, steep for 2 minutes, then remove them and keep warm.

2 Pour the broth through a sieve, then return it to the pan and reduce it somewhat. Stir in the cream continue to cook until the sauce has a creamy consistency. Season with salt and pepper to taste.

3 Cook the noodles until al dente according to the package instructions, then pour off the water and drain the noodles. Heat the butter in a large pan and toss the pasta in it.

4 Slice the scallops and briefly steep in the cream sauce. Place the noodles on warm plates and pour over the scallop sauce. Sprinkle with chopped parsley.

**Serves 4**

1 shallot

a few tarragon leaves

1 sprig each: fresh thyme, fennel leaf

7 tbsp/100 ml white wine

a few peppercorns

1 pinch saffron threads

16 fresh, shelled scallops

½ cup/125 ml cream

salt, freshly ground pepper

14 oz/400 g spinach noodles

2 tbsp/30 g butter

1 tbsp chopped parsley

*Prep. time: ca. 30 min.
(plus cooking time)
Per portion ca. 553 kcal/2323 kJ
25 g P, 15 g F, 76 g C*

# Spaghetti with Salmon & Lemon Sauce

Cook the spaghetti in a generous quantity of boiling water according to package instructions.

Cut the salmon first into strips, then into bite-sized pieces. Wash the dill, shake it dry, and finely chop.

In a saucepan, blend the egg yolks, lemon peel and juice, white wine, and sugar with a whisk. Add salt and pepper. Then reduce the heat to low and whip the sauce into a thick cream.

4 Cut the well-chilled butter into cubes and stir it into the sauce a little at a time. Fold in the dill and, if necessary, season the sauce to taste.

5 Drain the spaghetti and tip it back into the pot while it is still wet. Add the salmon pieces to the pasta and stir carefully for 3 minutes. Serve with the lemon sauce.

**Serves 4**

14 oz/400 g spaghetti
salt
11 oz/300 g salmon fillet
1 bunch fresh dill
4 egg yolks
grated peel of 1
untreated lemon
1 tbsp lemon juice
4 tbsp white wine
1 tsp sugar
pepper
8½ tbsp/120 g butter

*Prep. time: ca. 30 min.*
*Per portion ca. 706 kcal/2953 kJ*
*27 g P, 43 g F, 44 g C*

53

# Pasta with Tomatoes & Salmon

1 Wash and dry the arugula. Leaving the small leaves whole, either tear or coarsely chop the larger ones into pieces. Distribute the arugula among 4 plates. Cut the bacon in small cubes. Rinse the anchovies in cold water to remove some of the salt, dab dry, and chop finely.

2 Wash and dry the tomatoes and cut them in quarters. Cut out the flesh in the middle with the seeds and chop coarsely. Leave the pieces with skin as they are. Peel and finely dice the shallots and garlic. Rinse the salmon in cold water, dab it dry, and cut into cubes of ⅓–¾ in/1–2 cm.

3 Heat the olive oil in a large pan. Fry the bacon in it over medium heat until crispy. Cook the pasta until al dente, according to the package instructions. Add the shallots and garlic to the bacon and sweat until tranparent, then add the salmon and cook a further 2 minutes. Turn everything into a large, warm bowl.

4 Add the quartered and chopped tomatoes along with the sardines to the pan and briefly heat, then add to the salmon in the bowl. Combine the pasta with the salmon and tomatoes. Arrange on the arugula, season with pepper, and serve immediately.

**Serves 4**

3½ oz/100 g arugula
2–3 slices bacon
3 anchovy fillets
14 oz/400 g
cherry tomatoes
4 shallots
2 cloves garlic
¾ lb/350 g salmon fillets,
without skin
2 tbsp olive oil
salt
11 oz/300 g linguini
or spaghetti
pepper

*Prep. time: ca. 30 min.*
*Per portion ca. 463 kcal/1945 kJ*
*32 g P, 12 g F, 56 g C*

**Serves 4**

2¼ lb/1 kg mussels

2 shallots

2 tbsp olive oil

1 clove garlic

2 cups/500 ml
dry white wine

⅔ cup/100 g
vegetables for soup
(celery, carrot, and leek)

½ bunch dill

½ bunch parsley

salt, white pepper

9 oz/250 g tomatoes

14 oz/400 g fettuccine

1 bouquet garni
(e. g. thyme, bay leaf)

1 pinch sugar

1½ tbsp/20 g butter

a few saffron threads

2 tbsp chopped parsley

*Prep. time: ca. 45 min.
(plus cooking time)
Per portion ca. 442 kcal/1850 kJ
20 g P, 6 g F, 77 g C*

# Saffron Noodles
# with Mussels

1    Thoroughly clean the mussels under cold running water, discarding any that are open. Finely dice 1 shallot and sauté in 1½ tsp of the olive oil. Add half of the crushed garlic clove and the closed mussels, then pour in the wine and add water to cover.

2    Add the diced soup vegetables, the washed herbs, salt and pepper. Simmer, covered, for 8–10 minutes. Strain the broth and reduce it somewhat. Discard any mussels that have not opened. Remove the remaining mussels from their shells and keep them warm in the broth reduction.

3    Score the tops of the tomatoes, remove the stalks, blanch in boiling water, then skin and remove the seeds. Dice the tomato flesh.

4    Prepare the pasta according to package instructions, drain, and toss with 1 tbsp of the olive oil.

5    Heat the remaining 1½ tsp olive oil. Mince the second shallot and sauté it with the remaining crushed garlic. Add the tomatoes and bouquet garni to the pan and simmer over low heat. Remove the herbs, then season the sauce with salt, pepper and a pinch of sugar to taste.

6    Toss the fettuccine in butter. Add the saffron threads, the mussels and the tomato sauce to the pasta, and season again. Serve with a sprinkling of chopped parsley.

# Tortellini with Shrimp Filling

**Serves 4**

**2¼ cups/300 g flour**

**4 eggs**

**1 tbsp oil**

**salt**

**1 bunch scallions**

**1 piece ginger (ca. 1 in)**

**2 cloves garlic**

**¾ lb/350 g shrimp, cooked and shelled**

**1 tbsp soy sauce**

**1 red chili**

**1 red pepper**

**2 tbsp spiced sesame oil**

*Prep. time: ca. 50 min.*
*(plus resting time)*
*Per portion ca. 468 kcal/1966 kJ*
*34 g P, 12 g F, 56 g C*

1  Knead the flour, 3 eggs, oil and a little salt into a smooth, supple dough. Cover the dough in plastic wrap and let it rest for about 30 minutes.

2  Wash, rinse and dry the scallions and cut them into fine rings. Peel and finely grate the ginger. Peel the garlic and crush them in a mortar with some salt. Wash, dry, and chop the shrimp into small pieces.

3  Mix everything together, add the remaining egg, and season with the soy sauce and salt to taste.

4  Place the pasta dough on a flat, work surface sprinkled with flour and roll out until very thin. Use a pastry wheel or knife to cut out squares of about 2 in/5 cm. Place a teaspoon of shrimp filling in the middle of each square, then fold over into triangles. Press the edges together firmly and shape into tortellini.

5  In a large pot, bring a generous quantity of salted water to a boil and cook the tortellini for 5–8 minutes.

6  Cut the chili and bell peppers in half, trim, wash and remove their seeds. Finely dice both peppers. Heat the sesame oil in a pan, sauté the peppers, and season with salt and pepper. Serve the tortellini topped with the pepper mixture.

# ettuccine with Shrimp & Peppers

Halve, trim, wash, and finely dice the pepper. Peel and
[di]ce the onion and garlic. Heat the butter and sauté all the
[veg]etables for about 3–5 minutes.

Pour on the white wine and lobster stock and cook over
[high] heat for 2–4 minutes. Season with salt, pepper, and paprika
[to t]aste, and then stir in the crème fraîche.

3   Wash and dry the shrimp, then season with salt and pepper.
Heat the chili oil and brown the shrimp well on all sides. Add this
to the sauce and steep for about 3 minutes.

4   Cook the pasta in ample salted water until al dente,
according to the package instructions. Wash and dry the oregano,
pluck the leaves, and cut them into thin strips. Allow the pasta to
drain. Arrange on plates and top with the pepper and shrimp sauce.
Serve with a sprinkle of oregano.

**Serves 4**
2 red peppers
1 onion, 1 clove garlic
1 tbsp butter
⅓ cup/75 ml white wine
generous ¾ cup/200 ml
lobster stock
salt, pepper
paprika
2 tbsp crème fraîche
7 oz/200 g cooked shrimp
1 tbsp chili oil
11 oz/300 g
spinach fettuccine
½ bunch oregano

*Prep. time: ca. 30 min.*
*Per portion ca. 360 kcal/1512 kJ*
*20 g P, 5 g F, 55 g C*

57

# Spaghetti with Clams & Pesto Sauce

**Serves 4**

2 bunches basil

1 clove garlic

3 tbsp/30 g pine nuts

5 tbsp olive oil

salt

freshly ground pepper

14 oz/400 g spaghetti

14 oz/400 g clams
in the shell

1 tbsp lemon juice

*Prep. time: ca. 45 min.*
*Per portion ca. 440 kcal/1848 kJ*
*20 g P, 7 g F, 23 g C*

1   Wash and dry the basil, then pluck the leaves and mince them. Peel the garlic and chop it and the pine nuts into fine pieces. Combine everything in a small bowl and mix with 3 tbsp of the olive oil, salt, and pepper.

2   Cook the spaghetti according to package instructions until al dente. Allow to drain briefly, then turn it in a very large bowl that has been warmed.

3   Wash the clams and let them drain. Discard any open cla In a large pan, heat the remaining oil with the lemon juice. Add clams, cover the pan, and cook for just a few moments, until th clams open.

4   Discard any clams that have not opened. Blend the spagh with the pesto and clams and serve immediately.

# Tagliatelle with Clams in White Wine

**Serves 4**

2¼ lb/1 kg clams

2 shallots

1 pickled anchovy fillet

2–3 cloves garlic

5 tbsp olive oil

1/2 bunch flat parsley

4 oregano twigs

1 cup/250 ml
dry white wine

14 oz/400 g tagliatelle

salt, white pepper

*Prep. time: ca. 45 min.*
*Per portion ca. 519 kcal/2172 kJ*
*18 g P, 16 g F, 72 g C*

1   Thoroughly wash the clams in cold water and let drain. Throw away any open clams. Peel and dice shallots finely. Chop the sardine fillets finely. Peel garlic and put it through a press, then mix with the sardines and 1 tbsp olive oil. Wash and dry the parsley and oregano, then pluck and chop coarsely.

2   Heat remaining olive oil in a pan and adding the shallots, brown over a medium heat. Add sardine and garlic mixture and pour in the white wine.

3   Add clams, cover and steam over a medium heat, until the clams have opened. Uncover, throw out any closed clams and ad the chopped herbs. Cook for a further 5 minutes over a very low heat, stirring, repeatedly.

4   Cook pasta shells until al dente in ample salted water, according to package instructions. Pour out pasta and let drain. Season clams with salt and pepper and mix with drained pasta.

# Spaghetti with Clams in Tomato Sauce

**Serves 4**

2¼ lb/1 kg fresh clams

1 tbsp lemon juice

⅓ cup/80 ml olive oil

3 cloves garlic, crushed

ca. 2 lb/850 g peeled
tomatoes (canned)

salt, pepper

14 oz/400 g spaghetti

4 tbsp finely chopped
flat-leaf parsley

*Prep. time: ca. 25 min.*
*(plus cooking time)*
*Per portion ca. 580 kcal/2420 kJ*
*42 g P, 35 g F, 55 g C*

1   Thoroughly wash the clams and discard any that are open. Put them in a large pot, add the lemon juice, and add enough water to cover them. Cover the pot and simmer about 7–8 minutes, until the clams open. Discard any that are still closed. Remove the clams from the open shells and set aside.

2   Heat the olive oil in a large pan and sauté the garlic for 5 minutes. Stir in the tomatoes with their liquid. Bring to a boil, then cover and let simmer for 20 minutes. Season to taste with salt and pepper and heat the clams in the sauce.

3   Cook the spaghetti until al dente according to package instructions, then drain it and return it to the pot. Carefully stir in the clams and tomato sauce, top with the parsley, and serve.

59

# Linguine with Sardines

1   Wash and dry the sardine fillets, then cut them into pieces. Trim and rinse the fennel, then use a grater to slice it thinly. Peel the garlic and cut into thin slices. Wash and dry the chili and cut it into fine dice.

2   Heat 2 tbsp of the olive oil and sauté the garlic and chili in it. Add the sliced fennel and sauté about 5 minutes, then blend in the sardines. Cook another 4 minutes.

3   Cook the linguine in ample salted water until al dente, according to the package instructions. Drain the pasta. Mix the lemon peel and lemon juice, pine nuts, parsley, and salt and pepper to taste into the sardines. Add the remaining olive oil to the pasta and toss carefully.

**Serves 4**
**8 filleted sardines**
**1 fennel bulb**
**2 cloves garlic**
**½ red chili pepper**
**4 tbsp olive oil**
**¾ lb/350 g linguine**
**salt**
**grated peel of**
**1 untreated lemon**
**1 tbsp lemon juice**
**2 tbsp roasted pine nuts**
**3 tbsp chopped**
**fresh parsley**
**pepper**

*Prep. time: ca. 30 min.*
*(plus cooking time)*
*Per portion ca. 458 kcal/1924 kJ*
*23 g P, 12 g F, 62 g C*

# Tagliatelle with Smoked Salmon

1   Cook the pasta in ample salted water until al dente, according to the package instructions. Pour off the water and drain the pasta. Wash and dry the dill. Coarsely chop 2 of the sprigs.

2   Heat the cream with the vermouth and 1 sprig of dill until thick. Remove the dill and season the sauce with salt, cayenne pepper, and black pepper. Slice the salmon and stir into the sauce with the chopped dill. Mix the pasta and sauce and serve.

61

**Serves 4**
**14 oz/400 g**
**black tagliatelle**
**salt**
**3 sprigs dill**
**2 cups/500 ml cream**
**2½ tbsp/40 ml vermouth**
**cayenne pepper**
**pepper**
**14 oz/400 g**
**smoked salmon**

*Prep. time: ca. 30 min.*
*Per portion ca. 855 kcal/3591 kJ*
*35 g P, 47 g F, 73 g C*

# Pasta & Meat

Hearty pasta meals that include meat and poultry—which, when flavored with various herbs, make the most delicious sauces—are among the most satisfying foods imaginable. This chapter includes everything from easy yet elegant recipes with meatballs or salami to specialties resulting from the combination of pasta and game. Beef, rabbit, lamb, and poultry: all are inviting with pasta!

# Rigatoni with Lamb Ragout

**Serves 4**

9 oz/250 g lamb meat, leg or shoulder

salt, pepper

4 tbsp olive oil

2 cloves garlic

1 small red chili pepper

1 bay leaf

1 red and 1 yellow pepper

2 tbsp tomato paste

3½ tbsp/50 ml white wine

14 oz/400 g rigatoni

*Prep. time: ca. 30 min.
(plus cooking time)
Per portion ca. 523 kcal/2197 kJ
32 g P, 10 g F, 72 g C*

1 Cut the lamb into small cubes and rub with salt and pepper. Heat the olive oil in a pot and sauté the garlic cloves in it, then remove the garlic from the oil. Add the meat and fry until it begins to brown. Add the chili pepper and bay leaf.

2 Wash and deseeds the peppers, cut them into strips, then add to the meat. Stir the peppers and meat for a few moments, then add the tomato paste and wine. Cover and braise for 1 hour over low heat, until the meat is tender. If needed, add some m broth or water to the pot. Season to taste with salt and pepper remove the chili pepper and bay leaf.

3 Cook the rigatoni in ample salted water until al dente, according to the package instructions. Drain the pasta and serve it in warm bowls with the ragout.

**Serves 4**

1 red and 1 green pepper

1 bunch chervil

¾ lb/350 g boneless
chicken breast

2 tbsp oil

½ tbsp/20 g butter

½ cup/125 ml chicken broth

1 clove garlic

1–2 tsp paprika powder

1 tsp herbes de Provence
(e.g., rosemary, sage,
thyme, marjoram)

14 oz/400 g fettuccine

salt

7 tbsp/50 g freshly
grated Parmesan

cayenne pepper

*Prep. time: ca. 40 min.*
*Per portion ca. 686 kcal/2870 kJ*
*41 g P, 18 g F, 88 g C*

# Fettuccine with Chicken & Pepper Ragout

1  Quarter the peppers, remove the pith and seeds, and place them skin side up in a 390 °F/200 °C oven until the skin begins to blister. Then remove, let cool, discard the skins and finely dice the peppers.

2  Rinse and dry the chervil and pluck off the leaves. Cut the chicken breast into slices about ¾ in/2 cm thick.

3  Fry the chicken in hot oil over high heat for 2 minutes on each side, then remove it and keep warm. Heat the butter in a pan and add the peppers, sauté briefly, then add the broth and scrape the bottom of the pan to include all the browned chicken.

4  Peel and press the garlic cloves. Add the paprika, pressed garlic, and herbs de Provence to the pan and simmer for another 2 minutes, uncovered.

5  Cook the fettuccine in ample salted water until al dente, according to the package instructions. Pour off the water, and while still hot, combine the pasta with the sauce, chicken breast, and just over half of the grated Parmesan. Season generously with salt and cayenne pepper. Sprinkle with chervil and the rest of the Parmesan.

# Penne with Salami & Cheese

Remove the skin from the salami. Peel the onion. Cut both salami and onion into strips, and peel the garlic cloves.

Heat the oil in a large pan and fry the onions until they are transparent. Press the garlic into the pan. Add the salami strips and cook them quickly; they should not dry out. Pour in the wine and let it evaporate over a high heat.

3 Score the tops of the tomatoes, blanch with boiling water, skin, remove the seeds, and dice the flesh. Add it to the salami in the pan. Add the rosemary sprig and season with salt and pepper. Let this simmer over medium heat for 30 minutes. Finally, cut the cheese in strips (for example, provolone) and add to the sauce. It should melt. Do not let the sauce boil anymore.

4 Cook the penne in salted water until al dente according to package instructions. Allow the pasta to drain, then tip it into the sauce in the pan. Combine everything together for 1–2 minutes over low heat and stir in half the Parmesan cheese. Serve sprinkled with the remaining Parmesan.

**Serves 4**

**7 oz/200 g salami**

**1 large onion**

**2 cloves garlic**

**4 tbsp oil**

**7 tbsp/100 ml dry white wine**

**generous 1 lb/500 g ripe tomatoes**

**1 sprig rosemary**

**salt**

**freshly ground pepper**

**1½ lb/700 g firm cheese**

**14 oz/400 g penne**

**7 tbsp/50 g freshly grated Parmesan**

*Prep. time: ca. 30 min. (plus cooking time)*
*Per portion ca. 843 kcal/3541 kJ 71 g P, 57 g F, 6 g C*

67

# Fettuccine with Bacon

1 Cut the bacon into small cubes. Peel and finely chop the onion and garlic. Heat the olive oil in a pan and fry the bacon thoroughly. Add the onion and garlic and cook 2 minutes more.

2 Add the broth and parsley, then season with salt and pepper. Over a low heat, cook the mixture until it is reduced by half.

3 Wash the basil leaves, shake dry and chop finely. After the sauce has been reduced, stir in the chopped basil.

4 Cook the fettuccine in boiling salted water until al dente, then pour off the water, rinse the pasta, and let drain. Serve the fettuccine topped with bacon sauce and sprinkled with cheese.

**Serves 4**

**3½ oz/100 g bacon**

**1 onion**

**1 clove garlic**

**3 tbsp olive oil**

**⅔ cup/150 ml beef broth**

**1 tbsp chopped fresh parsley**

**salt, pepper**

**4 basil leaves**

**14 oz/400 g fettuccine**

**3½ oz/100 g pecorino cheese, shaved**

*Prep. time: ca. 20 min. (plus cooking time)*
*Per portion ca. 678 kcal/2840 kJ 48 g P, 52 g F, 6 g C*

# Pappardelle with Chicken Liver

**Serves 4**

generous 1 lb/500 g chicken livers

11 oz/300 g mushrooms

2 small red chilies

8 large sage leaves

1 untreated orange

1 tsp sugar

9 tbsp/140 ml olive oil

2 cloves garlic

salt

20 basil leaves

generous 1 lb/500 g pappardelle

1 tbsp balsamic vinegar

Prep. time: ca. 30 min.
(plus cooking time)
Per portion ca. 902 kcal/3771 kJ
47 g P, 37 g F, 86 g C

1   Rinse the chicken livers, remove any tendons or connective tissues, and cut the liver into bite-sized pieces. Trim and quarter the mushrooms. Cut the chili peppers in half, remove the seeds and finely dice the pods. Rinse the sage leaves, dry, and cut into thin strips.

2   Thinly peel the orange and cut the peel into julienne. Over low heat, melt the sugar until it is golden brown, then add the orange peel and cook until softened. Stir together the orange peel, diced chilies, sage, half the olive oil, the pressed garlic and a little salt.

3   Sauté the mushrooms in 4 tbsp olive oil over high heat f about 1 minute, then add salt and the orange peel mixture. Rin the basil leaves, shake dry and coarsely shred the leaves (reser few for garnish).

4   Cook the pasta in ample salted water until al dente, according to the package instructions. Drain the pasta. Dab the chicken liver dry. Fry in the remaining olive oil over high heat for about 2 minutes, add salt, and deglaze the pan with the vinegar

5   Add the mushroom mixture, chicken livers, and basil to th pasta, adjust the seasoning, and garnish with the remaining basi

# Chicken Liver with Penne

**Serves 4**

¾ lb/350 g chicken livers

generous 1 lb/500 g penne

1 onion

2 cloves garlic

3½ tbsp/50 g butter

2 tbsp grated orange peel

2 bay leaves

½ cup/120 ml red wine

2 tbsp tomato paste

2 tbsp cream

Prep. time: ca. 15 min.
(plus cooking time)
Per portion ca. 720 kcal/3010 kJ
33 g P, 20 g F, 90 g C

1   Rinse the livers. Remove any tendons or connective tissue. Cut each liver into bite-sized pieces.

2   Cook the pasta in ample salted water until al dente, according to the package instructions. Let it drain and keep warm. Peel the onion and garlic, and dice the onion.

3   Melt the butter in a pan and lightly sauté the onion. Press the garlic into the pan and add the liver, orange peel, and bay leaves. Sauté, stirring, for 3 minutes. Remove the chicken liver from the pan and stir in the red wine, tomato paste, and cream. Let it simmer until the sauce reduces and thickens.

4   Remove the bay leaves. Return the chicken liver to the pan and briefly warm it up. Season with salt and freshly ground pepper to taste. Pour the sauce over the pasta and serve.

# Spaghetti with Bratwurst, Lentils & Spinach

**Serves 4**

14 oz/400 g fresh spinach

1 small onion

1 tbsp oil

4 fresh bratwurst

9 oz/250 g spaghetti
or other thin pasta

salt

½ cup/100 g red lentils

½ cup/125 ml beef
or vegetable broth

½ cup/125 ml cream

freshly ground pepper

*Prep. time: ca. 40 min.
(plus cooking time)
Per portion ca. 840 kcal/3528 kJ
35 g P, 52 g F, 59 g C*

1 Clean the spinach, removing any hard stems. Rinse the leaves and place them in a pot while still dripping wet. Set the pot on the stove and over high heat let the spinach wilt. Shake the pot vigorously a few times while it does so.

2 Let the spinach cool slightly, then chop it coarsely. Peel and finely chop the onion. Heat the oil in a pan and sauté the onion over low heat until it is translucent. Press the meat out of the sausage skins, form it into meatballs, and add to the pan. Over medium heat, fry until the meat is brown all over. Cook the pasta until al dente according to package instructions, then drain.

3 Add the lentils to the pan with the meat and cook together for about 1 minute, stirring constantly. Add the spinach. Pour in the broth and cream, bring briefly to a boil, then cover the pan and simmer another 5 minutes over low heat. Season to taste with salt and pepper. Combine the pasta and meatballs with the spinach and serve in a hot serving dish.

# pinach Fettuccine with Prosciutto
## 1 Celery Cheese Sauce

Peel, rinse, and chop the celeriac into large cubes. In a large , bring to a boil an ample amount of water, salt and 2 tbsp of lemon juice. Add the celeriac, return to a boil, and cover the . Over medium heat, cook about 10 minutes until it is tender.

2 Remove the celeriac with a skimmer. Return the water the stove, bring to a boil, and use it to cook the pasta according package instructions.

3 In a second pot, combine the celeriac, milk, cream, and Gorgonzola and bring just to a boil, stirring constantly. Pureé to form the sauce. Heat the sauce, but do not allow it to boil. Season with the remaining lemon juice, salt, pepper, and nutmeg.

4 Drain the pasta briefly and combine it with the sauce while still very hot. Divide it between warm plates. Tear the ham slices into strips and arrange on the pasta along with the olives.

**Serves 4**

generous 1 lb/500 g
celeriac (celery root)

salt

3 tbsp lemon juice

9 oz/250 g wide fettuccine

7 tbsp/100 ml milk

7 tbsp/100 ml
whipping cream

2½ oz/75 g
Gorgonzola cheese

freshly ground pepper

freshly grated nutmeg

2½ oz/75 g shaved
Parma ham (prosciutto)

3½ oz/100 g black olives,
pitted

*Prep. time: ca. 30 min.
(plus cooking time)
Per portion ca. 445 kcal/1869 kJ
19 g P, 19 g F, 49 g C*

71

# Ravioli with Spinach & Sage Butter

1 Thoroughly combine the ingredients for the pasta dough. Cover the dough and let it rest for 20 minutes.

2 For the sauce, peel and chop onion and garlic, then rinse the rosemary and mince it as well. Heat the olive oil in a pan and sauté the onion, garlic, and rosemary. Add the ground beef to the pan and cook 5 minutes, stirring often. Stir in the remaining seasonings and the wine and let everything simmer together for 10 minutes.

3 Cull and wash the spinach, then while still wet, put it in a saucepan over medium heat let it wilt. Tip it into a colander to drain, pressing out any excess water. Finely chop the spinach and add it to the ground beef. Remove the bay leaf. Pureé this mixture, then work in the eggs, breadcrumbs, and Parmesan. Season with salt, pepper and nutmeg to taste.

4 Sprinkle flour on a flat work surface and roll out the dough into two thin, flat sheets. Place small scoops of filling at 1 in/ 3 cm intervals on one of the sheets of dough, then place the second layer of dough over it. Press the edges together. Now use a pastry wheel or knife to cut the dough between the filling in wide strips, and then to cut out ravioli.

5 Cook the ravioli in plenty of boiling salted water for about 4 minutes and then remove.

6 Melt the butter in a pan. Cut the sage leaves in thin strips and heat them in the butter. Serve the ravioli with the sage butter and sprinkled with Parmesan.

**Serves 4**

**For the pasta dough:**
2¾ cups/400 g flour
4 eggs
1 tsp salt
1 tbsp olive oil

**For the sauce:**
1 onion
1 clove garlic
1 tbsp fresh rosemary needles
2 tbsp olive oil
11 oz/300 g ground beef
1 bay leaf
½ tsp marjoram
½ tsp oregano
7 tbsp/100 ml dry white wine
generous 1 lb/500 g fresh spinach
4 eggs
7 tbsp/50 g breadcrumbs
2 tbsp freshly grated Parmesan
salt, pepper, nutmeg
7 tbsp/100 g butter
2 tbsp chopped sage leaves

*Prep. time: ca. 40 min.*
*(plus resting and cooking time)*
*Per portion ca. 868 kcal/3644 kJ*
*45 g P, 37 g F, 85 g C*

# Pasta with Duck Sauce

**Serves 4**

1 duck with innards

2 cups/500 ml red wine

1 each: carrot, leek, celery rib

1 onion

a few peppercorns

salt

1 small zucchini

1 carrots

2 tbsp olive oil

3½ tbsp/50 g butter

2 oz/50 g black olives, pitted

generous 1 lb/500 g pasta

*Prep. time: ca. 40 min.*
*(plus cooking time)*
*Per portion ca. 640 kcal/2688 kJ*
*24 g P, 19 g F, 90 g C*

**74**

1    Rinse the duck. Using a sharp knife, carefully remove the bone and skin from the duck breasts. Sever the legs and set them aside to use for another dish. Chop the remaining carcass into coarse pieces and place them in a soup pot.

2    Add the innards (without the livers), red wine and 1 cup/250 ml water to the pot. Trim the vegetables and cut into coarse pieces. Peel and quarter the onion. Add them to the soup pot with the peppercorns and salt, and let boil uncovered about 1 hour. The liquid should be reduced to ½ cup/125 ml.

3    Trim the zucchini and peel the carrot, then cut both into long julienne. Blanch in salted water and then drain.

4    Heat the oil and fry the duck breasts, turning them frequently. The meat should remain pink inside. Season with sa... Let the meat cool, then cut it into thin strips. Pour the duck broth through a fine sieve into another pan. Crush the duck livers and cook briefly in the duck broth. Add butter in pieces. Cut the olive... in fine strips and add them to the sauce along with the duck me... and the vegetables, and warm through briefly.

5    Cook the pasta in ample salted water until al dente, according to the package instructions. Drain the pasta, then serve with the duck sauce.

# Pappardelle with Wild Duck

**Serves 4**

1 each: carrot, leek, celery rib, onion

2 prepared wild ducks

2 tbsp olive oil

2 cups/500 ml dry white wine

1 can puréed tomatoes

1 cup/250 ml duck broth

1 bouquet garni

11 oz/300 g pappardelle

a little arrowroot to bind

1 tsp fennel seed

2 tbsp freshly grated Parmesan

*Prep. time: ca. 40 min.*
*(plus cooking time)*
*Per portion ca. 400 kcal/1680 kJ*
*18 g P, 11 g F, 55 g C*

1    Clean or peel the carrot, leek, celery, and onion and cut them into small pieces. Rinse the ducks, dab dry, then brown it in the hot olive oil in a pressure cooker with the diced vegetables. Add the white wine and puréed tomatoes.

2    Cook briefly and reduce slightly, then pour in the duck broth. Let the liquid come to a boil briefly, cover the pressure cooker, allow to steam for a few moments, then adjust the cooking level. The cooking time averages about 20 to 25 minutes (according to the size of the ducks).

3    When the cooking time is up, release the steam from the pressure cooker and open it. Remove the duck and quickly rinse it under cold water. Remove the meat from the bones and keep it warm.

4    Add the bouquet garni to the duck broth and simmer until it is reduced. Cook the pappardelle in salted water until al dente, according to package instructions. Remove the bouquet garni, strain the sauce, and if necessary, bind with arrowroot.

5    Divide the pasta onto warm plates, top with duck meat, and pour over the sauce. Serve with fennel seed and grated Parmesan sprinkled on top.

# Penne with Veal Ragout

**Serves 4**

1¼ lb/600 g veal

1 large onion

5 oz/150 g parsley root

7 oz/200 g portobello
mushrooms

5 tbsp olive oil

salt, pepper

1 tsp thyme

generous ¾ cup/200 ml
veal broth

¾ lb/350 g penne pasta

1–2 tsp flour

generous ¾ cup/200 ml
cream

1 cup/150 g frozen peas

1–2 tbsp lemon juice

Worcestershire sauce

½ bunch parsley, chopped

*Prep. time: ca. 30 min.*
*(plus cooking time)*
*Per portion ca. 790 kcal/3318 kJ*
*47 g P, 35 g F, 72 g C*

76

1  Rinse and pat dry the veal, then cut it in cubes. Peel the onion and parsley root. Dice the onion and slice the parsley root. Trim the mushrooms and cut into pieces as needed.

2  Heat half of the oil and sauté the mushrooms, stirring continuously, for 2–3 minutes. Remove the mushrooms and set them aside. Heat the remaining oil and fry the meat, stirring frequently.

3  Season with salt and pepper and add the onion and parsley root to the pan. Continue to cook for about 3 minutes, then add the thyme and veal broth to the ragout. Cover the pan and let simmer for about 45 minutes.

4  Near the end of that time, cook the pasta in ample salted water until al dente, according to the package instructions.

5  Uncover the ragout and let the liquid reduce a bit, then dust the flour over it and stir in the cream. Add the peas and mushrooms to the ragout and cook for about 5 minutes, stirring all the time.

6  Season the ragout with the lemon juice and Worcestershire sauce, salt and pepper to taste. Serve it with the penne, with a sprinkle of chopped parsley.

**Serves 4**

14 oz/400 g rabbit meat

2 oz/50 g pancetta
(Italian bacon)

1 onion

1 celery

1 carrot

1 beefsteak tomato

2 tbsp olive oil

salt, pepper

½ tsp dried thyme

7 tbsp/100 ml
dry white wine

½ cup/125 ml beef broth

14 oz/400 g pappardelle

*Prep. time: ca. 30 min.
(plus cooking time)
Per portion ca. 615 kcal/2583 kJ
21 g P, 23 g F, 76 g C*

77

# Pappardelle with Rabbit Ragout

1 Cut the rabbit meat into small pieces and finely dice the pancetta. Peel and chop the onion. Trim or peel the celery and carrot, then rinse and slice them. Cut a cross in the top of the tomato, blanch it in boiling water, remove the skin, and cut the tomato flesh into pieces.

2 Heat the oil in a pan and brown the diced bacon. Add the rabbit meat and fry well on all sides. Add the celery, carrot, and tomato and simmer together. Season with salt, pepper, and thyme. Stir in the wine and broth, cover the pan, and simmer the ragout over a low heat for about 1 hour and 20 minutes.

3 Toward the end of this time, cook the pappardelle in ample salted water until al dente, according to package instructions. Then pour off the water and allow the pasta to drain. Mix the noodles with the rabbit ragout and serve.

# arfalle with Meatballs & Cheese Sauce

Trim the broccoli and carrots. Peel the carrots and cut them small dice, and divide the broccoli into small florets. Cook broccoli and carrots in the broth over low heat, covered, for 6 minutes. Drain the broth, but retain it.

With damp hands, form the sausage into little balls. Fry in the hot oil until golden brown, about 2 minutes, then ove from the pan.

3 Peel and finely dice the onion, then sauté it in the fat left in the pan. Add 1 cup/250 ml of the broth to the onion along with the mascarpone and cornstarch. Stir with a whisk and let it come to a boil. Season with salt, pepper, and the lemon juice.

4 Rinse, dry, and chop the chervil. Add it to the sauce with the meatballs and the vegetables and heat everything through.

5 Cook the pasta according to package instructions in ample salted water until al dente, drain, and serve with the cheese sauce.

**Serves 4**
11 oz/300 g broccoli
11 oz/300 g carrots
1⅔ cups/400 ml
vegetable broth
7 oz/200 g veal sausage
3 tbsp oil
1 onion
7 oz/200 g
mascarpone cheese
1 tbsp cornstarch
salt, pepper
1 tbsp lemon juice
2 bunches chervil
¾ lb/350 g farfalle

*Prep. time: ca. 30 min.*
*(plus cooking time)*
*Per portion ca. 709 kcal/2970 kJ*
*25 g P, 37 g F, 68 g C*

**79**

# Spaghetti with Meatball Sauce

1 Peel the garlic cloves and onions and cut into fine dice. Trim he chili pepper, rinse, cut it in half, remove the seeds, and dice it nely. Heat the oil and briefly sauté the garlic, onions, and chili, tirring constantly. Add the tomato sauce and season well with salt, epper, and paprika to taste. Cover and let the sauce simmer for 0 minutes over a low heat.

2 Mix the two ground meats together. Knead in the egg and breadcrumbs and season thoroughly with salt, cayenne pepper, and paprika. Form balls out of the meat mixture and add them to the tomato sauce for about 10 minutes until they are cooked.

3 Cook the spaghetti in ample salted water until al dente, according to package instructions. Add the peas to the meatballs about 5 minutes before they are finished cooking.

4 Wash, dry, and finely chop the sage. Drain the spaghetti, rinse with cold water, and serve with the sauce. Garnish with a sprinkle of fresh sage and crumbled goat cheese.

**Serves 4**
1 clove garlic
2 onions
1 red chili pepper
3 tbsp olive oil
1 large can tomatoes
(for pizza sauce)
salt, pepper
hot paprika
5 oz/150 g ground lamb
5 oz/150 g ground beef
1 eggs, 2 tbsp breadcrumbs
cayenne pepper
14 oz/400 g spaghetti
⅔ cup/100 g frozen peas
½ bunch sage
3½ oz/100 g goat cheese

*Prep. time: ca. 35 min.*
*(plus cooking time)*
*Per portion  ca. 620 kcal/2604 kJ*
*38 g P, 17 g F, 77 g C*

**Serves 4**

9 oz/250 g venison

1 Spanish onion

1 carrot

generous 1 lb/500 g
white cabbage

½ bunch of chives

1 tbsp clarified butter

3½ oz/100 g bacon, diced

1 cup/250 ml dry red wine

½ cup/125 ml
venison or meat broth

1 tbsp tomato paste

1 tbsp thyme

pepper

1 tsp ground allspice

salt

14 oz/400 g rigatoni

*Prep. time: ca. 25 min.
(plus cooking time)
Per portion ca. 668 kcal/2804 kJ
21 g P, 49 g F, 28 g C*

# Venison Stew with Pasta

1 Wash and dry the meat and put it through a meat grinder. Peel and coarsely chop the onion. Trim, peel, and slice the carrot. Rinse the cabbage, remove the stalk, and cut into slices. Wash and dry the chives and cut into small rings.

2 Heat the clarified butter and render the bacon. Add the onion and sauté until translucent. Add the venison and brown well on all sides, stirring constantly. Then add the carrots and cabbage to the pan and combine everything well.

3 Blend the red wine and venison broth and pour into the pan. Season the meat with the tomato paste, thyme, pepper, allspice, and salt to taste and let it simmer for about 15 minutes over medium heat.

4 Cook the pasta until al dente according to package instructions, then pour off the water and let the pasta drain. Arrange the pasta and ragout in warm bowls and serve sprinkled with fresh chives.

# Spinach Fettuccine with Lamb

Rinse and pat dry the lamb, cut it into strips, and brown it [i]e hot oil. Season with salt and pepper, then remove the meat [f]m the pan.

Peel and finely dice the onion and garlic. Sauté both in the [sa]me pan in which the lamb was cooked. Add the vegetable broth [and] cream and bring to a boil.

Add the lentils and cook, uncovered, over medium heat for [... m]inutes. Stir in the cornstarch and bring the sauce to a boil.

4 Cook the fettuccine in ample salted water until al dente, according to package instructions.

5 Wash and dry the chives and cut them into small rings. Add them to the sauce along with the lamb. Season to taste with the lemon juice, salt, and pepper. Serve with the fettuccine.

**Serves 4**

generous 1 lb/500 g
rack of lamb

3 tbsp oil

salt

freshly ground pepper

1 onion

1 clove garlic

1 cup/250 ml
vegetable broth

1 cup/250 ml
whipping cream

½ cup/100 g red lentils

2 tbsp cornstarch

¾ lb/350 g
spinach fettuccine

1 bunch chives

1–2 tbsp lemon juice

*Prep. time: ca. 30 min.
(plus cooking time)
Per portion ca. 900 kcal/3768 kJ
42 g P, 47 g F, 77 g C*

81

## Tagliatelle with Prosciutto & Parmesan

**Serves 4**

**7 oz/200 g prosciutto**

**3 scallions**

**1 bunch basil**

**generous 1 lb/500 g
ripe tomatoes**

**2 tbsp/30 g butter**

**2 tbsp olive oil**

**14 oz/400 g tagliatelle**

**salt**

**scant 1 cup/100 g
grated Parmesan**

**freshly ground black pepper**

*Prep. time: ca. 30 min.
(plus cooking time)
Per portion ca. 779 kcal/3255 kJ
33 g P, 37 g F, 71 g C*

1 Cut the ham into narrow strips (about ⅓ in/1 cm wide). Trim and dice the scallions, only use the white portion.

2 Rinse the basil and shake it dry. Set aside a little for garnish and pluck the remaining leaves.

3 Wash and quarter the tomatoes, remove the stems, and dice the flesh in bite-sized cubes. Heat the butter and olive oil in a pan. Sauté the scallions until they are translucent.

4 Cook the tagliatelle until al dente according to package instructions, then pour off the water and let the pasta drain.

5 Add the ham strips to the scallions and mix together until the ham is warm.

6 Drain the tagliatelle. In a large bowl, layer the pasta with diced tomato, ham and scallion mixture, basil, and some of the Parmesan. Season with pepper, combine thoroughly, and garnish with the remaining basil leaves. Serve with crumbled Parmesan.

## Fettuccine with Beef & Mascarpone Sauce

**Serves 4**

**scant 1 cup/100 g walnuts**

**1¾ lb/750 g leeks**

**generous 1 lb/500 g
beef fillet**

**9 oz/250 g mascarpone**

**3 tbsp balsamic vinegar**

**salt**

**2 egg yolks**

**4 tbsp oil**

**white pepper**

**generous 1 lb/500 g
fettuccine**

*Prep. time: ca. 30 min.
(plus cooking time)
Per portion ca. 799 kcal/3341 kJ
36 g P, 43 g F, 62 g C*

1 Chop the walnuts coarsely. Trim and wash the leeks, then cut the white and light green parts into narrow rings.

2 Rinse and dry the beef. Cut the meat first in very thin slices and then in strips.

3 To make the sauce, whisk together the mascarpone, balsamic vinegar, and a little salt in a saucepan. Heat the mixture and beat in the egg yolks. The sauce should be hot but not come to a boil to prevent the egg yolk curdling.

4 Divide the oil between two pans and heat both of them. In one pan fry the beef strips a portion at a time in very hot oil for 1 to 2 minutes. In the other pan, sauté the leeks 4 to 5 minutes, stirring frequently, then mix in the walnuts. Season both the meat and leek with salt and pepper.

5 Cook the fettuccine in ample salted water until al dente, according to package instructions. Drain the pasta.

6 Combine the pasta with the leeks and beef strips and pour the mascarpone sauce over everything before serving.

# Fettuccine with Rabbit

**Serves 4**

14 oz/400 g fettuccine

salt

7 tbsp/100 g herb butter

2 cloves garlic

16 vineyard snails

1 tbsp chopped
flat-leaf parsley

5 tbsp cream

freshly ground pepper

2 rabbit legs

oil for browning

2 sprigs rosemary

2 rabbit fillets

4 rabbit kidneys

2 rabbit livers

**For the sauce:**

7 tbsp/100 ml veal broth

7 tbsp/100 ml cream

3½ tbsp/50 g
black olive paste

3½ tbsp/50 g chilled butter

3 tbsp whipped cream

*Prep. time: ca. 30 min.
(plus cooking time)
Per portion ca. 795 kcal/3339 kJ
41 g P, 39 g F, 71 g C*

1   Cook the fettuccine in ample salted water until al dente. Let the pasta drain. Melt the herb butter in a pan. Peel the garlic and press it into the pan. Halve the snails and add them as well, letting the butter foam. Gently fold in the pasta and chopped parsley. Add the cream and heat to just less than a boil. Season to taste with salt and pepper, then set it aside. Preheat the oven to 390 °F/200 °C.

2   Prepare the rabbit legs. Trim and discard any tendons, salt the meat, and brown it in a pan with a little hot oil and the rosemary. Then bake the legs for about 12 minutes in the oven. Season the rabbit fillets and add to the legs after 5 minutes. After another 4 minutes, add the halved and seasoned kidneys and livers. Remove the rabbit from the oven and let it stand 5 minutes.

3   For the sauce, bring the veal broth and cream to a boil a let it reduce by half. Add the olive paste and stir until smooth. Remove the pan from the heat and beat in the chilled butter in small pieces. Before serving, fold the whipped cream into the sauce. Arrange the pasta on warm plates and pour snail butter o it, then briefly place under a hot broiler.

4   Remove the meat from the rabbit legs and cut it in small pieces. Arrange the pasta, rabbit leg meat, fillets, kidneys, and livers on plates. Pour some of the olive sauce over the meat and serve with the remaining sauce.

# Spaghetti with Prosciutto

1 Soak the morels in lukewarm water. Cook the spaghetti in ample salted water until al dente according to package instructions. Peel and dice the onion.

2 Wash the tomatoes, score the tops, blanch in boiling water, skin them, and dice the flesh. Remove the morels from the water, rinse well, and let them drain.

3 Heat the butter in a pan and sauté the morels with the onion and tomatoes. Season with salt and pepper.

4 Wash the liver, dab it dry, and dice. Add to the pan with the tomatoes and cook together for about 8 minutes. Salt and pepper.

5 Remove the liver and keep it warm. Pour the mushroom broth into the pan and let the sauce reduce until creamy. Cut the prosciutto slices into strips and stir into the sauce. Drain the spaghetti and serve it with the sauce and the liver, garnished with freshly grated Parmesan and fresh marjoram leaves.

**Serves 4**

¾ oz/20 g dried morels

14 oz/400 g spaghetti

salt; 1 onion

4 tomatoes

4 tbsp butter

freshly ground pepper

¾ lb/350 g turkey liver

7 tbsp/100 ml
mushroom broth

4 slices bresaola
(air-dried beef)

⅔ cup/70 g
grated Parmesan

fresh marjoram to garnish

*Prep. time: ca. 30 min.
(plus cooking time)
Per portion ca. 778 kcal/3268 kJ
41 g P, 29 g F, 75 g C*

# Pasta & Vegetables

These recipes highlighting delicious combinations of vegetables and pasta are hits, and not only with vegetarians. From A for Asparagus to Z for Zucchini, this chapter features a wide range of delicious vegetables that are at their best when combined with pasta. Each recipe is crafted to highlight the vegetables' characteristic flavors. Look for freshness and quality when shopping for the ingredients—the results are worth it!

**Serves 4**

1 red and 1 yellow pepper

3 carrots

11 oz/300 g broccoli

1 bunch flat-leaf parsley

1 bunch basil

10 sorrel leaves

1 bunch scallions

7 oz/200 g spaghetti

salt

8 tbsp olive oil

3 tbsp lemon juice

pepper

*Prep. time: ca. 45 min.*
*Per portion ca. 411 kcal/1722 kJ*
*10 g P, 22 g F, 44 g C*

88

# Spaghetti Primavera

1 Cut the peppers in quarters, remove the seeds, and wash and dry the peppers. Place them under a preheated oven broiler with the skin side up until the skin turns black and blisters. Let them steam in a bowl covered with a damp cloth for 10 minutes, then remove the skins and cut the peppers into thin strips.

2 Peel the carrots and cut into very thin slices. Divide the broccoli into very small florets. Wash the parsley and basil, shake dry, and pull off the leaves. Coarsely chop both with the sorrel. Clean the scallions and slice them finely.

3 Cook the spaghetti in ample salted water until al dente, according to the package instructions. In the last 4 minutes, add the carrots and broccoli to the same pot. Drain and mix in a bowl with the oil, lemon juice, pepper, scallions, and herbs. Add salt and pepper to taste and serve hot or cold.

# quash Spaghettini

Wash, trim and peel the squash. Grate the flesh. Quarter
red pepper, remove the seeds, wash and finely dice the pepper.
roast the sesame seeds in an ungreased pan, then remove
m the pan and set aside. Melt the butter in a pan. Briefly sauté
curry powder and diced pepper in the butter.

Pour the stock and cream into the pan and bring to a boil.
d the grated squash and cook uncovered for 3 minutes. Season
th the lemon juice, a pinch of sugar, salt, and pepper.

3 Cook the spaghettini in salted water according to the
package instructions. Drain and combine with the sauce in
a prewarmed bowl. Wash the parsley, shake dry, and chop it
coarsely. Mix the parsley and sesame seeds into the pasta.

**Serves 4**

**14 oz/400 g squash
(without rind)**

**1 red pepper**

**3 tbsp sesame seeds**

**2½ tbsp/40 g butter**

**1–2 tbsp mild curry powder**

**3½ tbsp/50 ml
vegetable stock**

**generous ¾ cup/200 ml
whipping cream**

**1 tbsp lemon juice**

**sugar**

**salt**

**pepper**

**14 oz/400 g spaghettini**

**1 bunch flat-leaf parsley**

*Prep. time: ca. 35 min.*
*Per portion ca. 643 kcal/2701 kJ*
*17 g P, 29 g F, 78 g C*

89

# Pappardelle with Artichoke Hearts

**Serves 4**

2 cloves garlic

2–3 dried chili peppers

7 tbsp/100 ml olive oil

1 can artichoke hearts

4 sprigs thyme

½ bunch basil

3½ oz/100 g
dried tomatoes in oil

14 oz/400 g pappardelle

salt

⅓ cup/50 g pine nuts

7 tbsp/50 g
grated Parmesan

*Prep. time: ca. 45 min.*
*Per portion ca. 809 kcal/3398 kJ*
*21 g P, 45 g F, 80 g C*

1  Peel and mince the garlic. Crumble the chilies. Heat 1 tbsp of the olive oil and sauté for 2–3 minutes, then remove from the heat. Add 2 tbsp olive oil to the pan and stir it in.

2  Drain the artichoke hearts in a sieve and cut them in half. Rinse and dry the thyme and basil, then pull off and chop the leaves. Dice the dried tomatoes. Cook the pappardelle according to the package instructions, drain, rinse under cold water, and drain again. Dry roast the pine nuts in an ungreased, coated pan until golden brown.

3  Heat the remaining 2 tbsp olive oil in a pan, add the artichoke hearts, and brown on all sides for 4–5 minutes. Add the tomatoes and pasta and cook together. Stir in the garlic oil and pine nuts and add salt to taste. Serve with basil, thyme, and freshly grated Parmesan.

# Macaroni with Broccoli

**Serves 4**

14 oz/400 g broccoli

1 tbsp almond slivers

1 onion

7 oz/200 g Gorgonzola

14 oz/400 g
elbow macaroni

salt

1 tbsp olive oil

½ cup/125 ml cream

pepper, nutmeg

1 small box cress

*Prep. time: ca. 35 min.*
*Per portion ca. 610 kcal/2565 kJ*
*22 g P, 37 g F, 49 g C*

1  Trim the broccoli, wash it and divide into florets. Dry roast the almond slivers in an ungreased pan. Peel and dice the onion. Break the Gorgonzola into pieces.

2  Cook the macaroni in ample salted water until al dente, according to the package instructions. In a second pot, blanch the broccoli florets in boiling salt water for about 2–3 minutes. Drain both, rinse them under cold water, and let drain.

3  Heat the olive oil and sauté the onion in it until it is translucent. Pour in the cream and bring just to a boil. Add the Gorgonzola pieces to the sauce and let them melt over low heat. Season the sauce with salt, pepper and nutmeg to taste. Add the broccoli and macaroni.

4  Carefully heat everything together. Wash the cress, dry it, and cut it from the plant. Garnish the macaroni with cress and roasted almonds and serve immediately.

# Fettuccine & Eggplant

1   Preheat the oven to 440 °F/225 °C. Trim, wash, and dry the eggplants. Spread half of the oil on one of the eggplants, prick it several times with a fork, and bake on the middle rack in the oven for about 30 minutes or until the skin turns black. Scrape the eggplant flesh out of the shell. Peel the garlic and shallot. Finely purée them in a mixer with the eggplant flesh, lemon juice, and olive oil. Stir in the yogurt and add salt and pepper to taste.

2   Cook the fettuccine in ample salted water until al dente, according to the package instructions. Cut the second eggplant in slices. Heat the remaining vegetable oil and lightly brown both sides of the eggplant slices in it.

3   Wash and dry the chives and cut them into small pieces. Drain the pasta, rinse them under cold water, and drain. Combine the pasta, eggplant, and ricotta. Pour the sauce over everything, sprinkle with the chives, and serve.

**Serves 4**
**2 eggplants**
**5–6 tbsp vegetable oil**
**1 clove garlic**
**1 shallot**
**2 tbsp lemon juice**
**4 tbsp olive oil**
**10 tbsp/150 g yogurt**
**salt**
**pepper**
**14 oz/400 g fettuccine**
**½ bunch chives**
**3½ oz/100 g ricotta cheese**

*Prep. time: ca. 20 min.*
*(plus cooking time)*
*Per portion ca. 443 kcal/1858 kJ*
*8 g P, 8 g F, 74 g C*

# Penne with Zucchini & Ricotta

1   Cook the penne in ample salted water until al dente, according to the package instructions. Wash and trim the zucchini, then blanch it in salted water for 2 minutes, rinse under cold water, and cut in slices. Peel and mince the garlic. Wash and dry the basil and cut it into strips.

2   Heat the oil in a pan and sauté the zucchini slices for 1 minute. Add the garlic. Mix the penne, zucchini, basil, ricotta, season with salt and pepper, and serve with grated Parmesan.

**Serves 4**
**14 oz/400 g penne**
**salt**
**2¼ lb/1 kg small zucchini**
**3 cloves of garlic**
**1 bunch basil**
**2–3 tbsp olive oil**
**1½ cups/350 g ricotta**
**pepper**
**6 tbsp/40 g
grated Parmesan**

*Prep. time: ca. 15 min.*
*Per portion ca. 658 kcal/2764 kJ*
*28 g P, 26 g F, 80 g C*

93

# Penne with Green Asparagus

**Serves 4**

1 bunch scallions

3 tbsp olive oil

14 oz/400 g pizza
tomatoes (canned)

salt, pepper

generous 1 lb/500 g
green asparagus

14 oz/400 g penne

½ bunch basil

1 tbsp butter

3 tbsp freshly grated
Parmesan

*Prep. time: ca. 30 min.
(plus cooking time)
Per portion ca. 423 kcal/1775 kJ
14 g P, 19 g F, 49 g C*

1 Trim and wash the scallions and cut them into small rings. Heat the olive oil in a pot and sauté the scallions. Add the tomatoes and simmer over medium heat for about 7 minutes, until the sauce thickens somewhat. Add salt and pepper to taste.

2 Wash the asparagus, trim the ends and peel the lower third of each stalk. Cut the asparagus into pieces about 1½ in/4 cm long, then cook it in boiling salted water until al dente. Remove and let it drain.

3 Cook the pasta until al dente in the same water used to cook the asparagus. Wash the basil, shake it dry, and cut the leaves in strips.

4 Add the butter to the sauce, stir in the asparagus and basil, and adjust the seasoning. Let the sauce simmer for about 3 minutes longer. Serve the penne with the asparagus sauce, sprinkled with Parmesan cheese.

# Fettuccine with Arugula

1 Mix the semolina, flour, salt, and a little water and knead into a smooth dough. Roll out the pasta dough thinly on a work surface covered with flour and cut into strips.

2 Place the noodles on a floured baking sheet, cover with a dishtowel, and let it dry a bit. Wash the tomatoes, score them across the top, remove the stalks, blanch in boiling water, and skin. Cut the flesh into pieces. Peel and dice the garlic and onion.

3 Heat the oil and briefly sauté the diced garlic and onion in it. Add the tomatoes, season with salt and pepper, and cook the sauce over low heat for about 10 minutes.

4 Wash and dry the arugula and chop it into coarse pieces. Add it to the sauce and warm it for 2–3 minutes. Cut the Gorgonzola into small pieces and grate the Parmesan.

5 Cook the pasta in ample salted water until al dente, then drain. Blend the fettuccine and sauce, sprinkle with Parmesan and Gorgonzola, and serve.

**Serves 4**

⅔ cup/100 g semolina

1⅓ cups/200 g flour

salt, pepper

14 oz/400 g beefsteak tomatoes

2 cloves garlic

1 onion

3 tbsp olive oil

generous 1 lb/500 g arugula

3½ oz/100 g Gorgonzola

7 tbsp/50 g freshly grated Parmesan

*Prep. time: ca. 45 min.*
*(plus resting and cooking time)*
*Per portion ca. 457 kcal/1919 kJ*
*20 g P, 15 g F, 5 g C*

# ettuccine with Spinach & Gorgonzola Sauce

Peel, dice and sauté the onions in the butter until they are translucent. Add the spinach, still frozen, cover the pan, and steam low heat for 10 minutes, stirring occasionally.

Cook the fettuccine in ample salted water until al dente, according to the instructions on the package.

3 Add the cream, white wine, and half of the Gorgonzola to the spinach and purée with a hand-held blender.

4 Generously season the sauce with salt, pepper, and nutmeg. Drain the fettucinne and serve with the sauce and the remaining Gorgonzola, cut in cubes.

**Serves 4**

8 onions
3½ tbsp/50 g butter
generous 1 lb/500 g frozen leaf spinach
14 oz/400 g fettuccine
salt
½ cup/125 ml whipping cream
3 tbsp white wine
5 oz/150 g Gorgonzola
pepper
freshly ground nutmeg

*Prep. time: ca. 30 min.*
*Per portion ca. 679 kcal/3838 kJ*
*83 g P, 31 g F, 71 g C*

# Orecchiette with Fava Beans

1 Cook the beans in lightly salted boiling water for 6 minutes. Drain, rinse with cold water, and drain again. Press the kernels out of the skins. Coarsely dice the pancetta. Peel and press the garlic. Pull the arugula, wash it, and spin it dry. Tear off leaves in bite-size pieces. Crumble the feta.

2 Cook the orecchiette in ample salted water until al dente, according to the instructions on the package. Fry the pancetta in the olive oil until crisp. Add the beans and garlic to the pan and season with salt and pepper.

3 Drain the orecchiette and mix with the remaining ingredients in a bowl. Sprinkle with coarsely ground pepper and serve.

**Serves 4**

generous 1 lb/500 g frozen fava beans
salt
7 oz/200 g thinly sliced pancetta (cured Italian bacon)
3 cloves garlic
2 bunches arugula
7 oz/200 g feta cheese
14 oz/400 g orecchiette
1 tbsp olive oil
pepper

*Prep. time: ca. 40 min.*
*Per portion ca. 649 kcal/2720 kJ*
*42 g P, 21 g F, 71 g C*

## Spaghetti with Fresh Mushrooms

**Serves 4**
1 lb/450 g spaghetti
salt
9 oz/250 g mushrooms
1 sprig rosemary
pepper
6 tbsp/80 g butter
⅔ cup/75 g grated Parmesan
2 tbsp canola oil

*Prep. time: ca. 10 min.
(plus cooking time)
Per portion ca. 648 kcal/2720 kJ
22 g P, 27 g F, 78 g C*

1 Cook the spaghetti in ample salted water until al dente, according to the package instructions, then rinse with cold water and drain.

2 Trim the mushrooms and clean with a brush. Wash again, if necessary, dry immediately, and slice the mushroom caps paper thin. Wash the rosemary and shake it dry. Pull the needles off the stem and finely chop them.

3 Mix the hot, drained pasta with rosemary, salt, pepper, butter and about 2 tbsp of the water in which the spaghetti was cooked. Stir in the grated Parmesan and serve on warmed plates. Spread the mushroom slices across the top, drizzle the oil over the top, and serve immediately.

## Tortellini with Mushroom Sauce

**Serves 4**
generous 1 lb/500 g tortellini
salt
7 oz/180 g mushrooms
1 small unwaxed lemon
4 tbsp/60 g butter
1 clove garlic, pressed
1⅓ cups/320 ml cream
1 pinch nutmeg
freshly ground pepper
3 tbsp freshly grated Parmesan

*Prep. time: ca. 25 min.
Per portion ca. 610 kcal/2570 kJ
17 g P, 50 g F, 50 g C*

1 In a large pot, cook the tortellini until al dente in ample salted water. Drain, them tip them back into the pot and keep warm. Trim and thinly slice the mushrooms. Grate the lemon peel.

2 Melt the butter in a pot and sauté the mushrooms over medium heat for 2 minutes. Add the garlic, cream, lemon zest and nutmeg, then season to taste with freshly ground black pepper. Stir in the Parmesan and let the sauce simmer for 3 minutes.

3 Pour the sauce over the pasta and mix carefully.

# Macaroni with Olive Paste

**Serves 4**

**14 oz/400 g macaroni**

**2½ oz/75 g marinated green olives**

**4 anchovy fillets in oil**

**1 clove garlic**

**6 tbsp olive oil**

**1 tbsp cognac**

**1 tbsp lemon juice**

**1 tsp dried oregano**

**salt, pepper**

**generous 1 lb/500 g beefsteak tomatoes**

**7 oz/200 g artichoke hearts (jar)**

*Prep. time: ca. 30 min.*
*Per portion ca. 510 kcal/2142 kJ*
*35 g P, 8 g F, 74 g C*

1 Cook the macaroni in ample salted water until al dente, according to the package instructions. Then drain the pasta.

2 Halve the olives and remove the pits. Rinse the anchovies thoroughly and pat dry. Peel the garlic and finely purée it with 2 tbsp of the olive oil.

3 Stir together 2 tbsp olive oil with the cognac, lemon juice, and oregano and combine with the olive-anchovy purée. Add salt and pepper to taste.

4 Score the tomatoes across the top, blanch in boiling water, remove the skin and seeds, and dice the flesh. Drain the artichoke hearts and quarter them.

5 Heat the remaining olive oil in a pan and briefly heat the tomatoes. Then stir in the artichoke hearts and season with salt and pepper.

6 Mix the pasta with the vegetables and warm briefly over low heat. Serve immediately with the olive paste.

# Tagliatelle with Morels

Soak fresh morels in cold water for 5 minutes, or soak dried morels in lukewarm water, covered, for 30 minutes. Thoroughly clean the morels one by one under running water to remove grit from every crevice. Cut large morels into halves or quarters. Let dry on a paper towel.

Heat the butter in a deep pan and braise the morels for minutes. Gradually add the cream and the Marsala and continue to cook until the consistency of the cream thickens. Season to taste with salt, pepper, and the lemon juice.

3 Cook the tagliatelle in ample salted water until al dente, according to the package instructions. Add the pasta to the morels in the pan, mix well, and serve on warm plates.

**Serves 4**
9 oz/250 g fresh or
1 oz/25 g dried morels
2 tbsp/30 g butter
1 cup/250 ml cream
1 tbsp Marsala wine
salt
freshly ground pepper
juice of ½ lemon
14 oz/400 g
fresh tagliatelle

*Prep. time: ca. 25 min.
(plus soaking time)
Per portion ca. 600 kcal/2520 kJ
15 g P, 28 g F, 71 g C*

# Fettuccine with Peppers & Lime

**Serves 4**

1 each: red, yellow,
and green pepper

1 red chili pepper

3 cloves garlic

½ bunch flat-leaf parsley

14 oz/400 g fettuccine

4–5 tbsp butter

salt

pepper

1 lime

*Prep. time: ca. 40 min.*
*(plus resting and cooking time)*
*Per portion ca. 529 kcal/2222 kJ*
*12 g P, 27 g F, 50 g C*

1   Halve the peppers, remove the seeds, and wash. Place them under the oven broiler with the skin facing up until the skins turn black and form blisters. Remove from the oven and cover with a moist towel to cool. Then discard the skin and cut the peppers into strips about ¾ in/2 cm wide.

2   Halve the chili pepper, remove the seeds, and cut into strips. Peel and slice the garlic. Wash, dry, and finely chop the parsley.

3   Cook the fettuccine in ample salted water until al dente, according to the package instructions.

4   Heat the butter in a pan and sauté the chili and garlic for 1–2 minutes. Add the pepper strips and season with salt and pepper. Stir in the chopped parsley.

5   Drain the pasta and serve with the peppers with wedges of lime and a little lime juice drizzled over the fettuccine.

# Spinach Fettuccine with Sage & Tomatoes

**Serves 4**

2¼ lb/1 kg tomatoes

6 cloves garlic

3 shallots

2 tbsp olive oil

salt, pepper

generous 1 lb/500 g
spinach fettuccine

1 small sprig rosemary

7 tbsp/100 g butter

20 fresh sage leaves,
finely chopped

scant 1 cup/100 g grated
or shaved Parmesan

*Prep. time: ca. 40 min.*
*(plus cooking time)*
*Per portion ca. 723 kcal/3037 kJ*
*27 g P, 26 g F, 94 g C*

1   Wash the tomatoes, score them across the top, blanch in boiling water, remove the skin and seeds, and cut the flesh into large pieces.

2   Peel 2 cloves of garlic and slice them thinly. Peel the shallots, dice finely, and sauté in the hot olive oil with the peeled garlic. Add the tomatoes and let this mixture simmer over low heat for 30 minutes. Season with salt and pepper.

3   Cook the fettuccine in ample salted water until al dente, according to the package instructions. Peel the remaining cloves of garlic and slice. Wash the rosemary, pluck the needles off the stems, and coarsely chop them. Heat the butter, add the sliced garlic, rosemary, and sage leaves and allow it to froth up once.

4   Serve the pasta on warm plates with the tomato sauce topped with the freshly grated or shaved Parmesan over it. Finally, pour the hot sage butter over the fettuccine and serve.

# ettuccine with Mushroom-Leek Sauce

Trim and wash the leek then cut it into fine rings. Trim, wash dry the mushrooms. Separate the mushroom caps from the ms and cut the caps into narrow strips and the stems into thin es.

Cook the fettuccine in ample salted water until al dente, ording to the package instructions. Then drain and keep warm.

3 Heat the butter in a large pan. Sauté the leek and mushrooms on high heat for about 5 minutes, stirring constantly. Season with salt, pepper and cayenne pepper. Pour the white wine and cream over it and let the sauce simmer for 6–8 minutes. Then add nutmeg to taste.

4 Mix the fettuccine with the sauce. Serve on warm plates topped with freshly grated Parmesan.

**Serves 4**
2 leeks
9 oz/250 g
**mixed mushrooms**
9 oz/250 g
**narrow fettuccine**
1 tbsp oil
salt
2 tbsp butter
**freshly ground pepper**
1 pinch cayenne pepper
½ cup/125 ml
**dry white wine**
1 cup/250 ml
**whipping cream**
freshly ground nutmeg
scant 1 cup/100 g freshly
grated Parmesan

*Prep. time: ca. 25 min.*
*Per portion ca. 583 kcal/2449 kJ*
*21 g P, 32 g F, 49 g C*

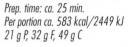

**105**

# Spinach Fettuccine with Mushroom Sauce

1 Wash, dry, and trim the mushrooms, then slice them. Peel, halve, and slice onions.

2 Cut the bacon into thin strips and render it in the oil in a pan. Add the onions and sauté until the onions are transparent.

3 Add the mushrooms to the pan and cook until the liquid has evaporated.

4 Cook the fettuccine in ample salted water until al dente, according to the instructions on the package.

5 Add the crème fraîche and bouillon to the pan with the mushrooms and simmer for 5 minutes, then season generously with salt and pepper to taste.

6 Wash, dry, and chop the basil, then mix it into the sauce. Serve the pasta and mushroom sauce sprinkled with Parmesan.

**Serves 4**
1¾ lb/750 g mushrooms
1¾ lb/750 g onions
5 oz/150 g bacon
1 tbsp oil
14 oz/400 g
**spinach fettuccine**
salt
3 cups/800 g crème fraîche
1 cup/250 ml bouillon
freshly ground pepper
1 bunch basil
7 tbsp/50 g freshly shaved
or grated Parmesan

*Prep. time: ca. 35 min.*
*Per portion ca. 850 kcal/3552 kJ*
*27 g P, 48 g F, 73 g C*

# Colorful Vegetable Spaghetti

**Serves 4**

2 carrots

1 zucchini

generous 1 lb/500 g
spaghetti

salt

1 unwaxed lemon

2 cloves garlic

½ bunch basil

1 ripe avocado

3 tbsp olive oil

1 tbsp cognac

pepper

10 tbsp/150 g sour cream

*Prep. time: ca. 35 min.*
*Per portion ca. 585 kcal/2457 kJ*
*18 g P, 15 g F, 92 g C*

1   Wash and peel the carrots. Trim, wash, and dry the zucchini. Thinly slice the vegetables lengthwise, then cut in thin strips.

2   Cook the spaghetti in ample salted water until al dente, pour off the water, and drain.

3   Rinse the lemon with hot water. With a zester, thinly slice off the peel. Peel and mince the garlic. Rinse and dry the basil, then chop it finely. Halve the avocado and remove the pit. Remove the flesh from its shell and mash it with a fork.

4   Heat the olive oil and sauté the garlic in it. Add the carrot strips, and after about 2 minutes the zucchini strips as well. Cook briefly, deglaze with the cognac, and add the avocado. Season with salt and pepper and stir in the sour cream. Toss the pasta in the vegetable sauce and serve on warmed plates. Garnish with basil and lemon zest and serve immediately.

# Shells with Vegetable Sauce

1 Wash the zucchini and eggplant. Cut off the stem ends. Cut the vegetables into thick slices, sprinkle with salt, and let draw for about 20 minutes.

2 Trim and wash the mushrooms. Dry thoroughly with a paper towel and slice them thinly. Rinse the sliced zucchini and eggplant and dry thoroughly as well.

3 Rinse the parsley, remove any bulky stems, and finely chop the rest. Peel and chop the garlic, then crush it with the broad side of a knife.

4 Heat the olive oil in a pan, briefly sauté the garlic and parsley, then add the zucchini, eggplant, and mushroom slices. Fry briefly, season the vegetables with oregano, salt, and pepper, and then cook slowly over low heat while stirring.

5 Cook the pasta in ample salted water until al dente, according to the instructions on the package.

6 Adjust the seasoning of the vegetables again, then combine them with the well-drained pasta shells and serve with freshly grated Parmesan.

**Serves 4**

**4 small zucchini**

**2 small eggplants**

**5 oz/150 g
fresh mushrooms**

**1 bunch parsley**

**1 clove garlic**

**3–4 tbsp olive oil**

**2 tsp oregano**

**salt**

**pepper**

**generous 1 lb/500 g
pasta shells**

**freshly grated Parmesan**

*Prep. time: ca. 30 min.
(plus drawing time)
Per portion ca. 545 kcal/2289 kJ
21 g P, 10 g F, 92 g C*

# enne with Wild Asparagus

Wash wild asparagus and cut off the lower ends. Wash
en asparagus, trim off the ends, and peel the lower third of
h stalk. Cut the asparagus on the diagonal into small pieces.
e the onion and ham.

Heat the butter in a large pan and fry the bacon and onion.
d the asparagus and chili pepper and fry them as well. Cook
e pasta in ample salted water until al dente, according to the
ckage instructions.

3 Add the cream and tomato purée to the pan with the
vegetables and let it reduce slightly. As soon as the sauce is
creamy, add the drained penne, season with salt and pepper, and
carefully blend everything together. Briefly heat it through once
more, then sprinkle with chopped parsley and serve.

## Serves 4

**generous 1 lb/500 g
wild or green asparagus**

**1 onion**

**2 oz/50 g uncured bacon**

**2½ tbsp/40 g butter**

**¼ dried chili pepper**

**11 oz/300 g penne**

**generous ¾ cup/200 ml
cream**

**1 tbsp tomato purée**

**salt**

**pepper**

**½ bunch parsley, chopped**

*Prep. time: ca. 30 min.
Per portion ca. 495 kcal/2079 kJ
16 g P, 22 g F, 57 g C*

109

# Tagliatelle with Cream Cheese & Broccoli Sauce

1 Clean broccoli and divide it into florets. Peel the stalk and
dice it. Cook the florets in the stock for 4 minutes, then drain,
reserving the stock.

2 Peel and finely dice the onions. Sauté them with the diced
broccoli stems in the melted butter. Pour 2 cups/500 ml of the
stock into the pan, cover, and cook for 8 minutes.

3 Cook the tagliatelle in ample salted water until al dente,
according to the instructions on the package.

4 Purée the broccoli stems in the stock. Stir in the cream
cheese and ¼ cup grated Parmesan, add the florets, and return to
a boil. Add salt and pepper to taste. Serve with the drained pasta,
coarsely ground pepper, and remaining Parmesan.

## Serves 4

**1¼ lb/600 g broccoli**

**2½ cups/600 ml
vegetable stock**

**1 onion**

**1 tbsp butter or margarine**

**11 oz/300 g fettuccine**

**salt**

**3½ oz/100 g cream cheese
with herbs**

**¼ cup + 3 tbsp/50 g
freshly grated Parmesan**

**pepper**

*Prep. time: ca. 25 min.
Per portion ca. 482 kcal/2024 kJ
20 g P, 20 g F, 55 g C*

## Linguine with Broccoli & Pistachio Cream Sauce

**Serves 4**

generous 1 lb/500 g broccoli

salt

1 shallot

2 tbsp olive oil

1⅔ cups/400 ml vegetable stock

10 tbsp/150 g crème fraîche

generous ¾ cup/100 g pistachios

1 tbsp lemon juice

pepper

2 tbsp capers

14 oz/400 g spinach linguine

*Prep. time: ca. 30 min.*
*Per portion ca. 680 kcal/2856 kJ*
*22 g P, 31 g F, 78 g C*

1 Trim and wash the broccoli and divide it into florets. Blanch the florets in lightly salted water for about 5 minutes, or until al dente. Then pour off the water, rinse under cold water, and drain. Peel and finely dice the shallot. Sauté the shallot in the hot oil until translucent. Coarsely chop one-quarter of the broccoli florets and add the pieces to the pan.

2 Stir in the vegetable stock and crème fraîche. Finely grind half of the pistachios and add them. Let everything come to a boil briefly, remove from the stove, and purée. Add the lemon juice and salt and pepper to taste. Stir in the remaining broccoli and half of the capers, mix everything together, and reheat.

3 Cook the pasta in ample salted water until al dente, according to the package instructions. Drain, then combine the linguine with the sauce and serve with the remaining capers and chopped pistachios.

**110**

## Sage Fettuccine

**Serves 4**

1¼ cups/150 g grated hard cheese

7 oz/200 g fettuccine

10 fresh sage leaves

2 tbsp butter

pepper

*Prep. time: ca. 25 min.*
*Per portion ca. 328 kcal/1378 kJ*
*18 g P, 12 g F, 35 g C*

1 Grate the cheese. Cook the fettuccine in ample salted water until al dente, according to the package instructions, then drain.

2 Wash and dry the sage leaves and cut them into thin strips. Heat the butter in a pan and sauté the sage in it.

3 Add the fettuccine to the sage in the pan and briefly combine them. Turn the buttered pasta into a warm bowl and toss with the grated cheese. Sprinkle with black pepper and serve.

# Pasta from the Oven

If the term "baked pasta" only brings to mind lasagna, you may be happily surprised by the wealth of delicious recipes in this chapter. All of the dishes included have two things in common. First, few foods please children more than pasta that has been baked in the oven, making these recipes guaranteed stress-free culinary delights for the whole family. In addition, all the recipes are easy to prepare, making them ideal for entertaining.

## Rolled Lasagna

**Serves 4**

**8 spinach lasagna noodles**

**salt**

**5 oz/150 g tuna fish (can)**

**1 bunch scallions**

**2 cloves garlic**

**1 bunch chervil**

**1⅔ cups/400 g quark
or ricotta**

**2 eggs**

**1½ cups/150 g freshly
grated Parmesan**

**pepper**

**butter**

*Prep. time: ca. 45 min.
(plus baking time)
Per portion ca. 493 kcal/2069 kJ
39 g P, 29 g F, 19 g C*

1 Cook the lasagna noodles in boiling salted water until al dente. Rinse under cold water, drain well, and set aside. Drain the tuna fish and break it into pieces with a fork.

2 Trim, wash, and dry the scallions then cut into thin rings. Peel and finely chop the garlic. Wash, shake dry, and finely chop the chervil. Mix together the quark or ricotta, eggs and 1 cup of the grated Parmesan. Stir in the scallions, garlic, and chervil and add salt and pepper to taste.

3 Preheat the oven to 355 °F/180 °C. Spread some of the filling on each of the lasagna noodles and roll them up. Cut the rolls into wide pieces and place them in a greased casserole dish. Sprinkle the rest of the Parmesan over them and bake in the middle rack of the oven for 15 minutes.

# Crispy Noodle Nests

Cook the spaghetti in ample boiling salted water until al ... Pour it into a sieve, rinse under cold water, and drain well.

Wash the tomatoes and remove the stems. Score the ...atoes across the top, blanch in boiling water, remove the skin ... seeds, and finely dice the flesh.

Wash and dry the arugula, then cut into thin strips. Dice the ... Peel and finely chop the garlic. Cut the fontina (or another ..., semi-soft cheese that melts well) into small cubes.

4 Preheat the oven to 390 °F/200 °C ... briefly fry the ham. Add the tomatoes, arugu... sauté together for a few moments. Season t... freshly ground pepper, and the paprika.

5 Form small nests out of the spaghetti ... greased baking dish. Fill the pasta nests with ... and scatter the cheese cubes over them. Bake... of the oven until the cheese has melted.

Ri...

**Serves 4**

7 oz/200 g rigatoni
salt
5 oz/150 g prosciutto
1 onion
2 cloves garlic
1 tbsp olive...
3½ oz...
3...

pepper
**1 tsp hot paprika**
**butter for the baking dish**

*Prep. time: ca. 45 min.*
*(plus baking time)*
*Per portion ca. 582 kcal/2447 kJ*
*35 g P, 24 g F, 55 g C*

115

# ...gatoni Gratin with Arugula

1 Cook the pasta in ample salted water until al dente, according to the package instructions. Pour into a sieve, rinse under cold water, and drain.

2 Cut the prosciutto into thin strips. Peel and mince the onion. Peel and press the garlic.

3 Heat the olive oil and sauté the onions until golden. Add the strips of prosciutto and garlic and swirl the pan to mix. Set aside.

4 Preheat the oven to 390 °F/200 °C. Crush the Gorgonzola and whisk it together with the eggs and cream. Season the cheese-cream sauce with salt, pepper, and freshly grated nutmeg.

5 Grease a baking dish. Combine the pasta with the prosci... and turn it in the dish. Pour the cheese-cream sauce over the p... and spread it out evenly. Bake on the middle rack of the oven... about 30 minutes.

6 Meanwhile, wash, dry, and tear the arugula into pieces. ... non-stick pan, dry roast the pine nuts until golden brown.

7 At the end of the cooking time, remove the Rigatoni Grat... from the oven and sprinkle the arugula over it. Grate or shave th... Parmesan onto the arugula and sprinkle the pine nuts over the t...

...oil

...100 g Gorgonzola

...ggs

1 cup/250 ml cream

pepper

freshly ground nutmeg

butter for the baking dish

7 oz/200 g arugula

3 tbsp pine nuts

7 tbsp/50 g freshly grated Parmesan

*Prep. time: ca. 30 min.*
*(plus baking time)*
*Per portion ca. 630 kcal/2646 kJ*
*25 g P, 43 g F, 38 g C*

**116**

# Spaghetti au Gratin

**Serves 4**
14 oz/400 g Swiss chard
7 oz/200 g
cherry tomatoes
2 onions, 2 cloves garlic
3½ oz/100 g aged Gouda
3 tbsp olive oil
salt, pepper
1 tsp rosemary needles
1 tbsp crushed, dried thyme
¾ lb/350 g spaghetti
2½ tbsp butter and
some for the baking dish

*Prep. time: ca. 45 min.*
*(plus baking time)*
*Per portion ca. 532 kcal/2234 kJ*
*20 g P, 21 g F, 64 g C*

1 Wash and dry the Swiss chard and tear it into pieces. Trim, wash, dry, and halve the cherry tomatoes. Peel and finely chop the onions and garlic. Coarsely grate the Gouda cheese.

2 Preheat the oven to 390 °F/200 °C. Heat the olive oil in a pan and sauté the onions and garlic until the onions are translucent. Add the Swiss chard to the pan and let it wilt, then add the tomatoes and cook them briefly while stirring. Season with salt and pepper, rosemary, and thyme.

3 Cook the spaghetti in ample salted water until al dente, according to the package instructions, then drain well.

4 Combine the spaghetti, the grated cheese and the vegetables. Grease a baking dish and spread the pasta and vegetable mixture in it. Dot the butter on the casserole and bake on the middle rack of the oven for about 20 minutes. Remove from the oven and serve immediately.

## Savoy Cabbage Lasagna

**Serves 4**

1 lb savoy cabbage, salt, 1 onion and 1 carrot, 2 tbsp olive oil, 14 oz ground beef, 1 tbsp dried thyme, pepper, 2 lb pizza tomatoes (canned), 2 tbsp butter, 4 tbsp flour, 2 cups white wine, ⅔ cup milk, 1 lb lasagna noodles, 1¼ cups ricotta, butter for the baking dish

*Prep. time: ca. 30 min. (plus cooking time)*
*Per portion ca. 1005 kcal/4221 kJ*
*56 g P, 42 g F, 96 g C*

1   Trim and wash the cabbage and cut it into strips. Blanch the cabbage in boiling salted water for about 5 minutes.

2   Prepare the ground beef mixture as described in Step 1, opposite, and combine it with the cabbage. Alternate layers of sauce, uncooked lasagna noodles, and crumbled ricotta in the greased baking dish and bake in the oven as indicated.

## Eggplant Lasagna

**Serves 4**

1½ lb eggplants, salt, 4 tbsp olive oil, 2 tbsp lemon juice, ½ bunch fresh basil (chopped), pepper, 1 onion, 14 oz ground beef, 1 tbsp dried thyme, 2 lb pizza tomatoes (canned), 2 tbsp butter, 4 tbsp flour, 2 cups white wine, ⅔ cup milk, 1 lb lasagna noodles, 9 oz Parmesan (grated), butter for the baking dish

*Prep. time: ca. 30 min. (plus cooking time)*
*Per portion ca. 1060 kcal/4452 kJ*
*59 g P, 47 g F, 95 g C*

1   Cook the eggplants in boiling salted water for 10 minutes. Drain, then cut lengthwise into slices. Blend 2 tbsp of the olive oil with the lemon juice, chopped basil, and some pepper and spread the seasoned oil on the eggplant slices.

2   Prepare the other ingredients as described opposite. Alternate layers of sauce, uncooked lasagna noodles, eggplant slices, meat mixture, and grated Parmesan in the greased baking dish and bake as indicated opposite.

## Lasagna with Mozzarella

**Serves 4**

1 onion, 1 carrot, 2 tbsp olive oil, 14 oz ground lamb, 1 tbsp dried sage, salt, pepper, 2 lb pizza tomatoes (canned), 2 tbsp butter, 4 tbsp flour, 2 cups white wine, ⅔ cup milk, 1 lb lasagna noodles, 7 oz Parmesan, 3 tomatoes, 7 oz mozzarella cheese, butter for the baking dish

*Prep. time: ca. 25 min. (plus cooking time)*
*Per portion ca. 1125 kcal/4725 kJ*
*67 g P, 52 g F, 94 g C*

1   Prepare the meat mixture and sauce as described in Step 1 and Step 2, opposite (using ground lamb instead of ground beef). Rinse the fresh tomatoes, remove the stalks, and slice. Cut the mozzarella into slices as well.

2   Fill the greased baking dish with alternating layers of sauce, lasagna noodles, lamb mixture, and freshly grated Parmesan. Finish with a layer of sauce. Place the tomato slices on top and cover with mozzarella. Bake in the oven as indicated opposite.

# ...sagna

Peel and chop or dice the onion and carrot. Heat the oil in ... and sauté the onion until it is translucent. Add the carrots ... ground beef and brown the meat well. Stir in the thyme and ...atoes and add salt and pepper to taste.

Melt the butter and stir in the flour to make a roux, then ...k in the white wine. Allow the sauce to reduce until thick and ...my, then stir in the milk and add a little salt. Preheat the oven ...90 °F/200 °C.

3 Spoon some of the sauce in the bottom of a greased baking dish. Place a layer of uncooked lasagna noodles on top, then spread some of the ground beef mixture on the pasta. Sprinkle some cheese over it. Repeat these layers until all of the ingredients have been used. The final layer should be sauce with cheese on top. Bake the Lasagna in the oven for about 40 minutes until it is golden brown. Serve garnished with fresh basil.

**Serves 4**

1 onion, 1 carrot
2 tbsp olive oil
14 oz/400 g ground beef
1 tsp dried thyme
2 lb/900 g pizza tomatoes (canned)
salt, pepper
2 tbsp butter
4 tbsp flour
2 cups/500 ml white wine
⅔ cup/150 ml milk
generous 1 lb/500 g lasagna noodles
2¾ cups/300 g grated cheddar
butter for the baking dish
basil to garnish

*Prep. time: ca. 40 min.*
*(plus cooking time)*
*Per portion ca. 1065 kcal/4473 kJ*
*55 g P, 50 g F, 94 g C*

119

# Macaroni Casserole with Venison

1 Peel and press the garlic. Wash, trim, and slice the zucchini. Mix the olive oil with 1½ tsp salt, freshly ground pepper, and the garlic and let the zucchini slices marinate in this for about 1 hour.

2 Wash and dry the venison and put it through the coarse setting of a meat grinder. Wash and halve the chili, remove the seeds, and cut the pod in thin strips. Finely dice the bacon. Peel the onion and carrot. Chop the onion and cut the carrot into julienne. Wash the tomatoes, remove the stalks, score the tops, blanch in boiling water, then skin and cut inhalf. Remove the seeds and dice the tomato flesh.

3 Heat the rosemary oil and render the bacon in it. Add the onion and carrots and briefly sauté. Add the venison and brown it thoroughly, stirring all the time. Then add the diced tomato and chili strips, and stew everything for about 10 minutes. Season with salt, freshly ground pepper, and the oregano. Cook the macaroni in ample boiling salted water until al dente, pour out the water, and drain well. Preheat the oven to 390 °F/200 °C.

4 Pour the stock into the pan with the meat-vegetable mixture and simmer, uncovered, until the liquid has evaporated. To make the cheese sauce, melt the butter, sprinkle the flour over it and stir briefly until smooth. Immediately pour in the warm milk and whisk with a wire whisk. Cut the cheese into large pieces and melt them in the sauce. Season with salt and pepper.

5 Grease a baking dish and cover the bottom with a layer of macaroni. Spread half of the meat sauce evenly over it. Cover with more macaroni, then place overlapping layers of the marinated zucchini over the pasta. Cover again with macaroni, then with the rest of the meat sauce. Add the last layer of macaroni and pour the cheese sauce over the entire dish and spread it evenly. Bake the casserole on the middle rack of the oven for about 30 minutes. Wash, dry, and finely chop the lovage and sprinkle it over the macaroni casserole just before serving.

**Serves 4**

2 cloves garlic
11 oz/300 g zucchini
½ cup/125 ml olive oil
1 tbsp salt
pepper
1¼ lb/600 g venison fillet
1 small chili pepper
5 oz/150 g slab bacon
1 onion
1 carrot
generous 1 lb/500 g
beefsteak tomatoes
2 tbsp rosemary oil
2 tsp crushed oregano
14 oz/400 g macaroni
2 cups/500 ml game
or beef stock
1 tbsp butter
1 tbsp flour
1 cup/250 ml milk, warm
2 oz/60 g kasseri
(hard sheep or goat cheese)
butter for the baking dish
3 sprigs lovage

*Prep. time: ca. 1 hour 15 min.
(plus cooking and marinating time)
Per portion ca. 540 kcal/2268 kJ
25 g P, 11 g F, 62 g C*

# Zucchini Fettuccine Casserole

**Serves 4**

generous 1 lb/500 g
zucchini

1 onion

1 clove garlic

9 oz/250 g cooked ham

7 oz/200 g fettuccine

7 oz/200 g red fettuccine

salt

1 tbsp butter

pepper

butter for the baking dish

¾ cup/80 g
grated Parmesan

¼ cup/30 g almond slivers

*Prep. time: ca. 35 min.*
*(plus marinating time)*
*Per portion ca. 593 kcal/2489 kJ*
*36 g P, 18 g F, 71 g C*

1   Trim and wash the zucchini. Cut each in two, then cut each half lengthwise and use a grater to cut each piece into thin slices. Peel and finely chop the onion and garlic. Dice the ham.

2   Cook the pasta in ample boiling salted water until al dente, according to the package instructions, then pour out the water and drain. Melt the butter and sauté the onion until transparent. Add the ham and zucchini and continue to sauté. Sprinkle the garlic on top and mix it in with the vegetables. Season with salt and pepper.

3   Grease a baking dish and put the fettuccine in it. Spread the zucchini-vegetable mixture over the noodles. Sprinkle on the Parmesan and spread it evenly across the top. Place under a preheated broiler until the cheese is golden brown.

4   Dry roast the almonds in an ungreased, non-stick pan until golden brown and sprinkle them over the casserole just before serving.

**Serves 4**

7 oz/200 g tagliatelle
salt
2 stalks celery
1 bunch flat-leaf parsley
3½ oz/100 g turkey
or chicken bologna
5 oz/150 g asparagus
sugar
6 artichoke hearts
marinated in oil
nutmeg, pepper
1 cup/120 g
grated Parmesan
butter for the baking dish
fresh parsley to garnish

*Prep. time: ca. 25 min.
(plus cooking time)
Per portion ca. 293 kcal/1229 kJ
18 g P, 17 g F, 17 g C*

# Noodle Casserole Carciofi

1 Cook the tagliatelle in ample boiling salted water until al dente, pour out the water, rinse under cold water, and drain well. Trim, wash and dry the celery and parsley. Cut the celery in half lengthwise and then into very small pieces. Finely chop the parsley. Cut the bologna into thin strips.

2 Wash and peel the asparagus. Cut off the ends and cut the stalks into pieces about ⅓ in/1 cm long. Briefly blanch the asparagus and celery in boiling water with a little sugar added, then drain. Drain the artichokes and cut into quarters.

3 Preheat the oven to 390 °F/200 °C. Grease a casserole dish. Combine the noodles with the bologna strips, celery, asparagus, and artichoke quarters. Season with ground nutmeg, pepper, and salt and spread into the casserole dish.

4 Sprinkle the freshly grated Parmesan over the casserole, then bake in the oven for about 30 minutes, or until golden brown. Then sprinkle with freshly chopped parsley and serve.

# aked Pasta with Meatballs

Cook the pasta in ample salted water until al dente, ording to package instructions. Pour off the water, drain, and with 1 tbsp of the oil.

Knead together the ground meat, egg, and quark or ricotta season with pepper. With moist hands, shape the meat into ut 15 meatballs. Wash and trim the zucchini. Cut lengthwise thin slices, reserve 10–12 slices, then dice the rest. Peel and ice the onion and garlic.

Brown the meatballs in 2 tbsp oil over medium heat for inutes or until browned all over, then remove them from the . Preheat the oven to 440 °F/225 °C.

4 Add 2 tbsp of oil to the pan and fry the zucchini, onion, and garlic in it. Add the tomato purée and cream and season with salt, pepper, and rosemary. Simmer for 3 minutes, uncovered.

5 Pour half of the sauce into an ovenproof casserole dish. Spread the pasta and meatballs over it and top with the remaining sauce. Arrange the reserved zucchini slices on top and brush with the remaining 1 tbsp of oil. Grate the cheese and sprinkle it over the casserole.

6 Bake the casserole on the middle rack of the oven for 15 minutes.

**Serves 4**

7 oz/200 g spiral pasta

salt

6 tbsp oil

11 oz/300 g ground pork

1 egg

2 tbsp lowfat quark
or ricotta

freshly ground pepper

3 zucchini

1 onion

1 clove garlic

14 oz/400 g pizza
tomatoes (canned)

⅔ cup/150 ml cream

2 tbsp rosemary needles,
chopped

½ cup/50 g grated
Emmantaler (Swiss) cheese

*Prep. time: ca. 35 min.*
*(plus cooking time)*
*Per portion ca. 720 kcal/3014 kJ*
*30 g P, 49 g F, 40 g C*

125

# Baked Macaroni Bolognese

1 Peel and finely dice the onions. Peel and press the garlic. Pluck off the rosemary needles and finely chop them.

2 Brown the ground beef with the onions, garlic, and rosemary in the hot oil for about 3 minutes. Crumble the ground beef and add the tomato purée. Season with salt and pepper and let simmer over medium heat, uncovered, for 10 minutes. Preheat the oven to 390 °F/200 °C.

3 Cook the pasta in ample salted water according to the instructions on the package. Pour out the water and drain briefly, then add it to the sauce and heat through.

4 Turn the pasta and sauce into a casserole dish. Sprinkle with the grated cheese and bake for 20–25 minutes in the preheated oven. Sprinkle with chives and serve.

**Serves 4**

2 onions

2 cloves garlic

2 small sprigs rosemary

¾ lb/350 g ground sirloin

2 tbsp oil

14 oz/400 g pizza
tomatoes (canned)

salt, pepper

7 oz/200 g bucatini
(long macaroni)

½ cup/50 g grated
Emmantaler (Swiss) cheese

1 tbsp chives

*Prep. time: ca. 25 min.*
*(plus cooking time)*
*Per portion ca. 390 kcal/1633 kJ*
*30 g P, 13 g F, 38 g C*

## Macaroni Casserole with Ham

**Serves 4**

generous 1 lb/500 g macaroni

salt

7 oz/200 g cooked ham

3½ oz/100 g Gouda

9 oz/250 g béchamel sauce

⅔ cup/150 ml milk

7 oz/200 g cream cheese

pepper

3 tbsp chopped chives

*Prep. time: ca. 20 min. (plus cooking time)*
*Per portion ca. 840 kcal/3528 kJ*
*42 g P, 33 g F, 92 g C*

1 Cook the macaroni in ample boiling salted water until al dente. Then pour out the water and drain.

2 Preheat oven to 440 °F/225 °C. Dice the ham and grate the Gouda. Bring the béchamel sauce and milk just to a boil, stir in the cheese, and season to taste with salt and pepper if desired. Alternate layers of pasta and ham in a greased baking dish, pouring the sauce over alternate layers.

3 Finally, spread the remaining sauce over the casserole, sprinkle with the grated cheese, and bake for 20 minutes in the hot oven. Sprinkle with the chives and serve.

## Baked Ravioli

**Serves 4**

11 oz/300 g fresh ravioli

salt

2 cloves garlic

½ bunch chervil

3 tbsp butter

4 carrots, grated

pepper

3½ oz/100 g aged Gouda

3 eggs

1 cup/250 ml milk

½ cup/125 ml cream

freshly grated nutmeg

butter for greasing

*Prep. time: ca. 20 min. (plus cooking time)*
*Per portion ca. 415 kcal/1743 kJ*
*21 g P, 29 g F, 17 g C*

1 Cook the ravioli in salted water until al dente, according to package instructions. Rinse under cold water and drain.

2 Peel and press the garlic. Wash, shake dry, and finely chop the chervil.

3 Preheat the oven to 390 °F/200 °C. Melt 2 tbsp of the butter and toss the grated carrot in it. Sauté for about 5 minutes then season with garlic, chervil, salt, and pepper. Grate the Gouda and whisk together with the eggs, milk, cream, nutmeg and salt.

4 Grease a casserole dish and alternate layers of ravioli and carrots. Pour the sauce over the top and spread it evenly. Bake on the middle rack of the hot oven for 40 minutes.

# Tortellini-Mushroom Bake

**Serves 4**

1¾ lb/800 g mushrooms

1 onion

2 cloves garlic

7 tbsp basil oil

2 tbsp crushed oregano

1¼ lb/600 g peeled
tomatoes (canned)

3 tbsp flour

1 cup/250 ml red wine

salt, pepper

11 oz/300 g tortellini

2 cups/250 g
grated Gouda

*Prep. time: ca. 30 min.*
*(plus cooking time)*
*Per portion ca. 550 kcal/2310 kJ*
*29 g P, 26 g F, 41 g C*

1 Trim and brush the mushrooms clean, then cut them into thick slices. Peel and finely dice the onion and garlic.

2 Heat 4 tbsp of the basil oil and sauté the onion and garlic in it until the onion is transparent. Stir in the oregano, then add the mushrooms and continue to sauté for 3 minutes, stirring. Drain the tomatoes and collect the juice. Dice the tomato flesh.

3 Dust the mushrooms in the pan with the flour, cook briefly, then deglaze with the red wine while stirring continuously. Add the diced tomatoes and their juice, and salt and pepper to taste. Cook for 10 minutes longer over medium heat.

4 Preheat the oven at 390 °F/200 °C. Cook the tortellini in ample boiling salted water until al dente, according to the package instructions. Then pour out the water, drain, and toss the tortellini in 1 tbsp oil.

5 Grease a large baking dish with 1 tbsp oil and spread half of the tortellini in the bottom of it. Spread half of the mushroom sauce and half the grated cheese over them. Repeat these layers with the remaining sauce and cheese. Finally, drizzle the remaining 1 tbsp oil over the casserole and bake for about 30 minutes on the middle rack of the hot oven.

# Tortellini Gratin with Vegetables

Cook the tortellini in ample salted water, according to the instructions on the package, until al dente. Tip into a sieve and drain well. Preheat the oven to 430 °F/220 °C.

Wash the zucchini, trim the ends, and grate it medium-fine on a vegetable grater.

Heat 2 tbsp of the butter in a pan and sauté the grated zucchini for 5 minutes over very high heat. Peel and press the garlic into the pan, and add salt.

4 Grease a casserole dish with the remaining butter. Spread the grated zucchini along the bottom and the tortellini over them.

5 Whisk the eggs with the milk, mix in the Parmesan, and season with salt and freshly ground pepper and nutmeg. Pour this mixture evenly over the gratin. Bake on the middle rack of the hot oven for 15 minutes, until the surface is golden brown.

**Serves 4**

generous 1 lb/500 g
**tortellini**
**salt**
14 oz/400 g **zucchini**
3 tbsp **butter**
2 cloves **garlic**
3 **eggs**
1 cup/250 ml **milk**
scant 1 cup/100 g
**freshly grated Parmesan**
**freshly ground pepper**
**freshly grated nutmeg**

*Prep. time: ca. 20 min.*
*(plus cooking time)*
*Per portion ca. 720 kcal/3024 kJ*
*33 g P, 24 g F, 92 g C*

129

# Salmon Lasagna

**Serves 4**

11 oz/300 g spinach lasagna noodles

salt

11 oz/300 g salmon fillet

2 tbsp lemon juice

1 onion

1 clove garlic

3 tbsp butter

7 tbsp/100 ml white wine

1 cup/250 ml cream

pepper

grated peel of ½ lemon

3½ oz/100 g Gorgonzola

scant 1 cup/100 g grated pecorino

butter for the dish

3½ tbsp/50 g butter

fresh dill to garnish

*Prep. time: ca. 30 min.*
*(plus cooking time)*
*Per portion ca. 948 kcal/3981 kJ*
*37 g P, 63 g F, 41 g C*

1 Cook the lasagna noodles in boiling salted water for about 10 minutes until al dente. Rinse the salmon, pat it dry, sprinkle with the lemon juice and salt, then cut it into bite-sized cubes.

2 Peel and finely dice the onion. Peel and mince the garlic. Heat the butter in a pan and sauté the onion and garlic.

3 Add the salmon and stir briefly. Deglaze the pan with the white wine, then stir in the cream. Simmer until the sauce has thickened slightly and season with salt and pepper. Preheat the oven to 480 °F/250 °C.

4 Stir in the lemon peel. Crush the Gorgonzola with a fork and grate the pecorino cheese. Pour the water off the lasagna noodles and let them drain.

5 Butter an ovenproof baking dish and fill it with alternating layers of lasagna noodles and salmon sauce. Finish with a layer pasta on top.

6 Sprinkle both of the cheeses and dot the butter on the last layer. Bake the Salmon Lasagna on the middle rack of the oven about 15 minutes. Garnish with fresh dill and serve.

# Spinach Lasagna

**Serves 4**

4½ lb/2 kg leaf spinach

2 onions

1¼ lb/600 g tomatoes

1–2 cloves garlic

3½ tbsp/50 g butter

5 tbsp/40 g flour

1¼ cups/300 ml milk

1½ cups/350 ml cream

1 tbsp herbs de Provence

5 eggs

salt, pepper

11 oz/300 g fontina

12–15 lasagna noodles (no precooking required)

½ bunch flat-leaf parsley

*Prep. time: ca. 20 min.*
*(plus cooking time)*
*Per portion ca. 1013 kcal/4255 kJ*
*54 g P, 61 g F, 60 g C*

1 Cull and wash the spinach thoroughly, then blanch it in salted water for 5 minutes. Then rinse with cold water and press out as much liquid as possible. Peel and finely dice the onions. Wash, trim, and slice the tomatoes. Peel and press the garlic.

2 Heat the butter and cook the spinach and onions in it. Dust the flour over the pan, then add the milk and cream. Blend in the garlic and herbs and cook for 2 minutes. Remove from the stove and stir in the eggs. Season with salt and freshly ground pepper. Preheat the oven to 355 °F/180 °C.

3 Grate the fontina (or other mild, semi-soft cheese that melts well). Alternate layers of lasagna noodles, spinach, tomatoes and grated cheese in a shallow baking dish, with spinach and cheese as the final layers. Bake on the middle rack of the hot oven for about 50 minutes. Sprinkle the Spinsch Lasagna with the finely chopped parsley and serve.

# Macaroni Casserole with Kippers

**Serves 4**

7 oz/200 g
elbow macaroni

⅓ cup/80 g butter

3 tbsp/30 g flour

1 cup/250 ml milk

1 cup/250 ml cream

¾ cup/80 g grated
Emmentaler (Swiss) cheese

salt

pepper

1 tbsp chopped dill

1 tbsp chopped parsley

14 oz/400 g kippers

2 apples

juice of 1 lemon

*Prep. time: ca. 30 min.
(plus cooking time)
Per portion ca. 790 kcal/3318 kJ
37 g P, 47 g F, 55 g C*

1 Cook the elbow macaroni in ample salted water until al dente, according to the package instructions, then drain. Preheat the oven to 390 °F/200 °C.

2 Melt 3½ tbsp/50 g of the butter in a pan and sprinkle the flour, stirring continuously. Let it foam up once, then pour in the milk and cream. Stir thoroughly and let the sauce come to a good boil. Add ½ cup of the grated cheese and season with salt, pepper, and the chopped herbs.

3 Skin the fish, debone, and tear into small pieces. Peel and quarter the apples, remove the cores, then cut into slices. Combine the kippers and apples with the pasta, stir in the sauce, and season with salt, pepper, and lemon juice.

4 Turn the mixture into a greased baking dish, spread the remaining butter over it in small pieces, and bake on the middle rack of the oven for 20–30 minutes until golden brown.

**Serves 4**

2 slices toast

14 oz/400 g saltwater fish fillet

5 oz/125 g cooked shrimp

7 oz/200 g mussels (jar)

2 eggs

2 bunches watercress

salt, pepper, lemon juice

1⅓ cups/150 g shredded mozzarella

2 tbsp butter

3 tbsp flour

2 cups/500 ml milk

nutmeg

butter for the baking dish

11 oz/300 g cannelloni

generous 1 cup/125 g grated pecorino

*Prep. time: ca. 30 min.
(plus cooking time)
Per portion ca. 695 kcal/2919 kJ
57 g P, 30 g F, 48 g C*

# Seafood Cannelloni

1  Soften the slices of toast in warm water. Rinse, dry, debone and cut the fish fillet into chunks. Press the water from the toast and finely purée them with the fish in a food processor.

2  Rinse, drain, and chop the shrimp. Drain the mussels in a sieve and chop them as well. Add both to the fish purée and mix in the eggs.

3  Wash, dry, and finely chop the watercress. Set aside about 2 tbsp of the cress and stir the rest into the fish mixture. Season with salt, pepper, and lemon juice and add the grated mozzarella.

4  Preheat the oven to 390 °F/200 °C. Melt the butter and stir in the flour. Add the warm milk and bring to a boil, stirring continuously. Season the sauce with salt and nutmeg to taste.

5  Grease a shallow baking dish and spread some of the sauce on the bottom. Fill the cannelloni with the fish mixture and place them in the baking dish. Pour the remaining sauce over the cannelloni and sprinkle with the pecorino. Bake on the middle rack of the hot oven for 25–30 minutes. Remove from the oven and serve garnished with the remaining watercress.

# Savoy Cabbage Cannelloni

1   Trim and wash the cabbage. Cut out the stalk. Remove [ni]ce leaves and blanch them in a large pot of boiling water for [abo]ut 1 minute until they are soft enough to roll up. Remove with [a s]kimmer, rinse with cold water, and drain on a paper towel.

2   Cut out the thick center rib of the cabbage leaves and cut [the] remaining cabbage into fine strips. Add the oil and some salt [to t]he cabbage broth. Cook the lasagna noodles in it for about [x] minutes, in portions, until they can easily be rolled. Remove and [pla]ce them on paper towels to drain.

3   Heat half the butter in a large pan. Sauté the cabbage strips over medium heat for 5 minutes, stirring constantly. Season with salt, pepper, and nutmeg to taste and turn into a bowl to cool. In the meantime, lightly salt and pepper each of the whole cabbage leaves. Place 1 lasagna noodle and 1 slice of smoked pork on each and roll up into cannelloni.

4   Finely dice the mozzarella. Combine the cabbage strips, cream, egg, and mozzarella and turn it into a greased baking dish. Place the cannelloni close together on top of the cabbage. Melt the remaining butter. Brush the cannelloni with it and sprinkle the grated Parmesan over top. Cover the dish and place it in the cold oven. Bake around 40 minutes at 355 °F/180 °C.

**Serves 6**

1 small savoy cabbage
(ca. 1¼ lb/600 g)
salt
1 tbsp oil
12 lasagna noodles
4 tbsp/60 g butter
pepper
freshly ground nutmeg
12 thin slices smoked
pork chop
7 oz/200 g mozzarella
generous ¾ cup/200 ml
cream
1 egg
butter for the baking dish
¼ cup/30 g
grated Parmesan

*Prep. time: ca. 35 min.*
*(plus cooking time)*
*Per portion ca. 690 kcal/2898 kJ*
*38 g P, 38 g F, 50 g C*

# Romanesco Cannelloni

1   Trim, wash and dry the romanesco and cut it into small [fl]orets. Peel and finely dice the carrots. Trim, wash, dry and cut [t]he leek into thin strips. Heat the oil and sauté the vegetables for [a]bout 5 minutes while stirring. Remove from the heat and stir in [t]he sour cream and eggs. Season the mixture with salt, pepper, [n]utmeg, and lemon juice to taste.

2   Preheat the oven to 390 °F/200 °C. Melt the butter, stir in the flour, brown it slightly, then pour in the milk and bring to a boil. Add salt, nutmeg, and lemon juice to taste.

3   Grease a shallow baking dish. Spread some of the sauce on the bottom. Fill the cannelloni with the vegetable mixture and place them close together in the baking dish. Pour the sauce over the cannelloni and sprinkle with grated cheese. Bake on the middle rack of the oven for 20–25 minutes. Serve Romanesco Cannelloni sprinkled with fresh chives.

**Serves 4**

11 oz/300 g romanesco
11 oz/300 g carrots
1 leek
2 tbsp olive oil
6 tbsp/100 g sour cream
2 eggs
salt, pepper, nutmeg
lemon juice
2 tbsp butter
3 tbsp flour
2 cups/500 ml milk
butter for the baking dish
7 oz/200 g cannelloni
1 cup/100 g grated cheese
4 tbsp chopped chives

*Prep. time: ca. 30 min.*
*(plus cooking time)*
*Per portion ca. 385 kcal/1612 kJ*
*21 g P, 18 g F, 33 g C*

# Gardener-Style Cannelloni

**Serves 4**

generous 1 cup/150 g flour

generous 1 cup/150 g semolina

4 eggs

salt

generous 1 lb/500 g leaf spinach

3½ oz/100 g uncured bacon

4½ oz/125 g mozzarella

1 sprig oregano

2 cloves garlic

10 tbsp/150 g ricotta

pepper

butter for the baking dish

1 egg yolk

7 tbsp/50 g grated pecorino

5 tbsp olive oil

3 oz/80 g béchamel sauce

**136**

*Prep. time: ca. 50 min.*
*(plus resting and cooking time)*
*Per portion ca. 703 kcal/2955 kJ*
*38 g P, 32 g F, 53 g C*

1  Combine the flour, semolina, eggs and ½ tsp salt with 7 tbsp/100 ml lukewarm water and knead into a smooth dough. Cover the dough and let it rest for about 30 minutes. Cull, wash, drain, and briefly blanch the spinach. Cut the bacon into thin strips and dice the mozzarella.

2  Wash the oregano, shake it dry, and finely chop the leaves. Peel and press the garlic. Mix the ricotta and mozzarella with the spinach, bacon, oregano, and garlic. Salt and pepper generously to taste. Preheat the oven to 480 °F/250 °C.

3  Roll out the pasta dough very thinly (2 mm) and cut out 20 rectangles with side of about 4 in/10 cm. Cook the pasta, in portions, in a large pot of salted water. Remove and drain.

4  Lay the pasta rectangles on a work surface. Spread some of the spinach filling on each rectangle and roll them up, letting them rest seam side down. Brush a baking dish with butter.

5  Place the cannelloni in the dish. Whisk the egg yolk with the pecorino, oil, and béchamel sauce and spread this mixture over the cannelloni. Season with salt and pepper. Bake the cannelloni on the middle rack of the oven for about 20 minutes, or until the surface is golden brown.

**Serves 6–8**

1 tbsp rosemary needles

11 oz/300 g
thinly sliced bacon

4 tbsp oil

1⅓ cups/350 g
crème fraîche

6 eggs

salt, pepper

4½ lb/2 kg small, ripe
tomatoes

1¾ lb/750 g vermicelli

3½ oz/100 g Parmesan

1½ tbsp softened butter

3 tbsp/20 g breadcrumbs

3 tbsp olive oil

11 oz/300 g scallions

1 bunch basil

11 oz/300 g mild feta

11 oz/300 g
medium-aged Gouda

*Prep. time: ca. 1 hour 30 min.*
*Per portion ca. 1220 kcal/5114 kJ*
*43 g P, 83 g F, 75 g C*

# Vermicelli Casserole with Tomatoes

1 Wash and dry the rosemary needles and dry roast them in an ungreased pan over medium heat until slightly brown, then finely chop the needles. Finely dice the bacon and brown it in 2 tbsp of hot oil. Beat the crème fraîche and eggs in a bowl for 4–5 minutes with a hand mixer at the highest speed. Add salt and pepper, and stir in the bacon and rosemary.

2 Wash the tomatoes, score the tops, remove the stems, blanch in boiling water and remove the skin. Cut the tomatoes in half horizontally. Cook the pasta in ample salted water for just 3–4 minutes, drain, and toss with the remaining oil. Combine the pasta well with the egg mixture and half of the Parmesan. Preheat the oven to 390 °F/200 °C.

3 Grease a casserole or baking dish with butter and sprinkle with a thin layer of breadcrumbs. Spread half of the pasta mixture evenly in the dish. Set the lower halves of the tomatoes on the pasta, with the cut surface facing down, and lightly press them down. Cover with the rest of the pasta mixture. Place the remaining tomato halves on top and brush with olive oil.

4 Bake the casserole 35–40 minutes on the middle rack of the oven.

5 Wash and dry the scallions and basil and chop them separately, and not too finely. Dice the feta. Remove the rind from the Gouda and grate it coarsely. Let the casserole cool on a rack for 10–15 minutes. While still warm, cut into pieces and serve accompanied by the cheese and herbs.

# aked Spaghettini with Peppers

Wash, dry, trim, and dice the peppers into small cubes. Peel
press the garlic. Cut the mozzarella into slices.

Wash and dry the thyme. Pull off the leaves and roughly
them. Heat 2 tbsp of the olive oil in a large pan. Sauté the
pers thoroughly over medium heat, stirring frequently.

3 Add the garlic, lemon peel, and half of the thyme. Salt and
pepper to taste, and turn the mixture into a large bowl. Preheat the
oven to 480 °F/250 °C. Cook the spaghettini in ample salted
water until al dente, according to the instructions on the package.
Then pour off the water, drain, and mix the pasta with the peppers.

4 Turn everything into a baking dish, top with the mozzarella
slices, sprinkle with the rest of the thyme, and drizzle with the
remaining oil. Place in the hot oven and bake 8–10 minutes until
the cheese is melted and slightly brown.

**Serves 4**
**2 each: red, green,
and yellow peppers**
**2 cloves garlic**
**14 oz/400 g mozzarella**
**½ bunch thyme**
**3 tbsp olive oil**
**1 tsp grated lemon peel**
**salt**
**pepper**
**11 oz/300 g spaghettini**

*Prep. time: ca. 40 min.
(plus cooking time)
Per portion ca. 603 kcal/2533 kJ
31 g P, 26 g F, 59 g C*

139

# Pasta Salads

Whoever thinks of pasta salads as only ubiquitous party dishes will be surprised to find what wonderful ideas await. The palette of delights stretches from a green noodle salad with jumbo shrimp to a farfalle salad with red lentils to a pasta salad with mushroom tomato sauce, a refreshing summer main dish or an opulent winter appetizer, they are guaranteed to place a magical smile on your face. And for your next party you can surprise them all.

# Farfalle Salad with Red Lentils

**Serves 4**

½ cup/100 g red lentils

2 cups/500 ml beef stock

11 oz/300 g farfalle

salt

1 onion

3½ oz/100 g red beets
(from a jar)

1 carrot

1 leek

2 tbsp lemon juice

3 tbsp oil

pepper

2 tsp ground allspice

1 tsp paprika

5 oz/150 g beef jerky

1 bunch parsley, chopped

*Prep. time: ca. 25 min.
(plus cooling time)
Per portion ca. 403 kcal/1690 kJ
21 g P, 7 g F, 3 g C*

1   Rinse the lentils. In a large saucepan, cook the lentils in the beef stock for 10 minutes over low heat. Cook the pasta in ample salted water until al dente, according to the package instructions.

2   Peel and finely chop the onion. Cut the beets in strips. Clean and peel the carrot and cut into thin discs. Trim, wash, and slice the leek into thin rings.

3   Whisk the lemon juice with the oil and season with salt, pepper, allspice, and paprika. Cut the jerky in thin strips.

4   Drain the lentils and pasta in a colander, rinse with cold water, and drain again. Allow to cool completely. Then add the carrots, leek, onion, and jerky. Combine with the dressing, arrange on plates, and serve.

**Serves 4**

1 large eggplant

4 tbsp coarse sea salt

3 red peppers

2 medium zucchini

2 beefsteak tomatoes

14 oz/400 g mozzarella

½ bunch parsley, chopped

generous 1 lb/500 g mixed tortellini

salt

pepper

½ cup/125 ml olive oil

*Prep. time: ca. 30 min.
(plus standing time)
Per portion ca. 543 kcal/2278 kJ
47 g P, 24 g F, 33 g C*

143

# Tortellini Tricolore

1 Wash the eggplant and cut it in slices ¼ in/6 mm thick. Place the slices on a plate and sprinkle with the sea salt. Cover them with a clean towel, weight the top, and let stand for about 1 hour. After that time rinse and dry the eggplant, then cook under a hot oven broiler for 4 minutes on each side.

2 Clean, halve, and deseed the peppers, then cut them in strips. Wash the zucchini and cut it lengthwise in narrow strips. Score the tomatoes across the top, blanch in boiling water, remove the skins and seeds, and dice the flesh. Cut the mozzarella in cubes. Wash, dry, and finely chop the parsley.

3 Cook the tortellini according to the package instructions. Pour off the hot water, rinse in cold water, and drain well. Set aside to cool.

4 Cut the eggplant slices in half and combine with the rest of the vegetables and the mozzarella. Season with salt and pepper. Toss the vegetables with the parsley and drizzle with olive oil. Combine with the tortellini and serve.

144

# Warm Vegetable-Noodle Salad

Wash, quarter, and deseed the peppers. Place them on a baking sheet with the skin side up. Broil on the middle rack of the oven until the skin is black and blistered. Cover with a damp towel and allow to cool. Then peel the peppers and cut in strips.

Wash, peel and thinly slice the carrots. Wash the broccoli and separate into small florets. Cook the tagliatelle in salted water with 2 tbsp olive oil until al dente, according to the package instructions. Add the carrots and broccoli to the pasta for the last minutes of cooking. Drain everything, rinse with cold water, and drain and cool in a colander. Shake the pasta occasionally so that it does not stick.

3 Score the tomatoes across the top, remove the stems, blanch in boiling water, then remove the skins and seeds. Cut the tomato flesh into fine dice. Pull the leaves from all the herbs and wash them. Coarsely chop the parsley, thyme, and lemon balm; finely chop the mint and sage. Leave the basil leaves whole.

4 Heat the tomatoes and peppers in the rest of the olive oil, season with salt and pepper, mix with all the herbs and the tagliatelle, and serve immediately.

**Serves 4**
1 red and 1 yellow pepper
2 carrots
11 oz/300 g broccoli
5 oz/150 g tagliatelle
10 tbsp olive oil
salt
7 oz/200 g tomatoes
1 bunch flat-leaf parsley
½ bunch fresh thyme
1 small bunch lemon balm
2 stems fresh mint
8 small sage leaves
½ bunch basil
3 tbsp lemon juice
pepper

*Prep. time: ca. 50 min.*
*Per portion ca. 364 kcal/1521 kJ*
*8 g P, 21 g F, 32 g C*

145

# Warm Pasta Salad with Cherry Tomatoes

1 Wash the tomatoes, remove the stems, and cut in quarters. Dry roast the pine nuts in an ungreased pan until golden brown. Clean the zucchini and cut lengthwise in slices ¼ in/6 mm thick. Cut the slices diagonally into strips and salt them.

2 Pit the olives. Peel the garlic, slice it, then cut the slices in julienne and sauté in the hot oil until golden brown. Remove from the pan and drain on a paper towel. Dry the zucchini and sauté in the hot garlic oil for 2–3 minutes, stirring occasionally. Drain in a sieve, recapturing the oil.

3 Coarsely grate or crumble the feta. Wash and dry the basil leaves. Set a few aside and cut the rest in fine strips. Halve the chili, deseed, and wash and mince the pod. Make a dressing from the garlic oil, olive oil, vinegar, chili, and a little salt.

4 Break the tagliatelle into pieces about 2–2½ in/5–6 cm long and cook in ample salted water until al dente, according to package instructions. Drain well, then combine the pasta with the other ingredients and garnish with the reserved basil leaves before serving.

**Serves 4**
generous 1 lb/500 g
cherry tomatoes
⅔ cup/100 g pine nuts
11 oz/300 g zucchini; salt
3½ oz/100 g black olives
6 cloves garlic
4 tbsp oil
7 oz/200 g mild feta
1 bunch fresh basil
1 red chili
4 tbsp olive oil
2 tbsp red wine vinegar
9 oz/250 g
green tagliatelle

*Prep. time: ca. 1 hour*
*Per portion ca. 539 kcal/2257 kJ*
*17 g P, 35 g F, 34 g C*

**Serves 4**

11 oz/300 g jumbo shrimp

2 cloves garlic

4 tbsp orange juice

4 tbsp olive oil

salt

¾ lb/350 g green spaghetti

½ bunch lemon balm

4 tbsp crème fraîche

2 tbsp lemon juice

pepper

lemon wedges to garnish

*Prep. time: ca. 30 min.*
*(plus marinating time)*
*Per portion ca. 393 kcal/1649 kJ*
*24 g P, 5 g F, 62 g C*

# Green Pasta Salad with Jumbo Shrimp

1   Shell the shrimp, cut them open down the back, and remove the main vein. Rinse and dry. Peel and press the garlic.

2   Combine the orange juice, olive oil, and ⅛ tsp salt. Marinate the shrimp in this mixture for about 1 hour. Cook the spaghetti in a large pot of salted water until al dente. Pour off the water, rinse in cold water, and drain well.

3   Wash and dry the lemon balm and set aside a few leaves for garnish. Cut the rest of the leaves into fine strips. Mix the crème fraîche and lemon juice and season with salt and pepper. Blend in the strips of lemon balm.

4   Drain the shrimp and broil them for no more than 2 minutes per side. In a large salad bowl, combine the spaghetti with the salad dressing and top with the shrimp. Serve garnished with lemon balm leaves and the lemon wedges.

**Serves 6–8**

2 oz/50 g dried porcini

1½ cups/350 ml
white wine

1 large onion

5 cloves garlic

⅔ cup/150 ml olive oil

1 large can peeled
tomatoes (28 oz)

8 tbsp lemon juice

salt, pepper

generous 1 lb/500 g
chicken livers

11 oz/300 g spaghetti

2 bunches fresh basil

3 bunches flat-leaf parsley

generous 1 cup/120 g
grated pecorino

*Prep. time: ca. 1 hour 30 min.
(plus cooling and standing time)
Per portion ca. 507 kcal/2123 kJ
24 g P, 28 g F, 34 g C*

# Pasta Salad with Tomato-Porcini Sauce

1   Cook the porcini in ⅔ cup/150 ml of the wine until the liquid is almost completely evaporated. Allow the mushrooms to cool, then mince them.

2   Peel and finely dice the onion. Peel and press the garlic, and sauté both in 3 tbsp of the olive oil. Add the porcini, the remaining wine, the tomatoes with their juice, and the lemon juice. Cover the pan and simmer over low heat until the tomatoes disintegrate (about 30 minutes). Cool some, then add 7 tbsp/100 ml olive oil and season with salt and pepper.

3   Remove the membranes and connective tissue from the chicken livers and cut them in small cubes. Brown the chicken liver in portions in the remaining olive oil, over high heat, for about 2 minutes. Add each portion to the tomato sauce as it is ready. Let the sauce stand overnight.

4   The next day, cook the spaghetti in ample salted water until al dente, according to package instructions. Drain the pasta and add it to the cold tomato sauce while still hot. Mix well and season with salt and pepper. Leave the salad to draw at room temperature until ready to serve.

5   Shortly before serving, set a few basil leaves aside, chop the remaining leaves and the parsley, and mix with the salad. Garnish with whole basil leaves and freshly grated pecorino.

# asta Salad with Chicken

Thaw the peas. Cook the pasta in ample salted water with
sp oil until al dente, according to the package instructions. Pour
the hot water, rinse in cold water, and drain well.

Cut the chicken breast in strips. Heat the remaining 2 tbsp
n a skillet and brown the meat, turning frequently so that it is
enly cooked. Season with salt and pepper and allow to cool.

3 Wash the tomatoes and score them across the top. Blanch
briefly in boiling water, then remove the skins and seeds and cut
the flesh into fine strips.

4 Combine all the prepared ingredients. Mix the mayonnaise,
yoghurt, cream, ketchup, sherry and sugar. Season to taste with
salt and pepper. Blend the sauce with the salad ingredients and
allow to draw before serving.

**Serves 4**

**2 cups/300 g frozen peas**

**9 oz/250 g farfalle**

**4 tbsp oil**

**salt**

**11 oz/300 g
turkey breast fillet**

**pepper**

**4 tomatoes**

**3 tbsp mayonnaise**

**⅔ cup/150 g plain yoghurt**

**4 tbsp whipping cream**

**3 tbsp tomato ketchup**

**3 tbsp cream sherry
or port wine**

**1 pinch sugar**

*Prep. time: ca. 30 min.
(plus standing time)
Per portion ca. 580 kcal/2436 kJ
31 g P, 23 g F, 61 g C*

149

# Pasta Salad with Seafood

**Serves 4**

14 oz/400 g medium
shell pasta

1 cup/250 g mayonnaise

3 tbsp chopped
fresh tarragon

1 tbsp chopped
flat-leaf parsley

cayenne pepper

1 tsp fresh lemon juice

4 radishes

1 small red pepper

2¼ lb/1 kg cooked
assorted shellfish (shrimp,
lobster, crab, crayfish in
any combination) shelled
and cut in bite-sized pieces

*Prep. time: ca. 30 min.*
*Per portion ca. 598 kcal/2512 kJ*
*23 g P, 24 g F, 71 g C*

1 Cook the pasta shells in ample salted water until al dente, according to the package instructions. Drain, tip into a large bowl, and mix with 1–2 tbsp of the mayonnaise. Allow to cool to room temperature, stirring occasionally.

2 Thoroughly mix the tarragon, parsley, cayenne pepper, and lemon juice in a bowl with the remaining mayonnaise.

3 Wash and thinly slice the radishes. Wash the pepper, rem the seeds, and cut the pepper into thin strips.

4 Combine the shellfish, radishes, and pepper with the pas and season with salt and pepper to taste. Stir in the tarragon mayonnaise. Cover and keep cool until ready to serve. If the sc becomes dry, add a bit of lemon juice or mayonnaise.

**150**

# Smoked Salmon Pasta Salad

**Serves 4**

7 oz/200 g shell pasta

salt

1 cup/150 g frozen peas

1 tbsp oil

2 eggs

7 oz/200 g smoked salmon

10 tbsp/150 g
whole milk yoghurt

10 tbsp/150 g
crème fraîche

1 tsp grated lemon rind

3 tbsp lemon juice

pepper

sugar

½ bunch fresh dill, chopped

*Prep. time: ca. 30 min.*
*Per portion ca. 490 kcal/2054 kJ*
*25 g P, 24 g F, 44 g C*

1 Cook the pasta shells in ample salted water until al dente, according to the package instructions. Add the peas to the cooking water 2 minutes before the shells are finished. Drain the pasta and peas and mix with the oil. Hard-boil the eggs (10 minutes), rinse in cold water, then peel and cut each into six wedges. Cut the salmon in wide strips.

2 Mix the yoghurt, crème fraîche, lemon rind, and lemon and season with salt, pepper, and a pinch of sugar. Combine th pasta shells with the peas, eggs, salmon, and sauce and allow draw a short while. Sprinkle with dill and serve.

# Salmon & Rigatoni Salad

1 Dry roast the slivered almond in an ungreased pan, stirring constantly. Remove from the heat and set aside.

2 Wash the broccoli and divide it into florets. Peel the stem and cut it into small pieces.

3 Wash the parsley and add it to a saucepan containing the wine, ½ cup/125 ml water, 1 tsp salt, and the lemon slices. At the same time, bring 3 quarts of heavily salted water to the boil for the pasta.

4 Wash the salmon fillet, add it to the wine broth, cover the pan and cook over low heat for about 7 minutes.

5 Cook the pasta in the salted water until al dente. After 4 minutes add the broccoli stems to the pasta, and add the florets after another 2 minutes. Finish cooking the pasta and broccoli together, then drain, rinse in cold water, and drain thoroughly.

6 Remove the salmon from the broth and divide it into large pieces. Strain the broth through a sieve and reserve.

7 Melt the butter and skim off the foam. Pour in the fish broth, then add the saffron and boil over high heat until the sauce is reduced by one third. Remove the pan from the heat and allow to cool slightly.

8 Pour the sauce over the pasta-broccoli mixture and allow to draw until the pasta takes on an even gold color. Carefully mix the salmon into the pasta and season with salt and pepper. Strew with the slivered almonds and serve at room temperature.

**Serves 4**

2 tbsp slivered almonds

generous 1 lb/500 g broccoli

1 cup/250 ml dry white wine

salt

3 sprigs parsley

3 lemon slices

11 oz/300 g salmon fillet

11 oz/300 g rigatoni

7 tbsp/100 g butter

2 g saffron powder

pepper

*Prep. time: ca. 35 min.*
*Per portion ca. 605 kcal/2541 kJ*
*28 g P, 31 g F, 44 g C*

153

**Serves 4**

9 oz/250 g tortellini

salt

2 cups/300 g frozen peas

7 oz/200 g
canned pineapple

7 oz/200 g
canned mushrooms

1 cup/150 g canned corn

½ small red pepper

½ small green pepper

1 shallot

2–3 tbsp vinegar

4 tbsp sunflower oil

pepper

1 tbsp mixed chopped
salad herbs

pepper strips and parsley
to garnish

*Prep. time: ca. 20 min.
Per portion ca. 596 kcal/2490 kJ
17 g P, 23 g F, 68 g C*

# Colorful Tortellini Salad

1 Cook the tortellini in ample salted water until al dente, according to the package instructions. Pour off the hot water, rinse in cold water and drain. Cook the frozen peas, rinse in cold water, drain, and let them cool.

2 Cut the pineapple in small pieces and slice the mushrooms. Rinse the corn and let it drain. Trim, deseed and wash the peppers. Set aside a few strips and finely dice the rest. Peel the shallot and cut into thin rings.

3 Combine all the prepared ingredients. Whisk the vinegar oil together and season with salt, pepper and the herbs. Pour ov the salad ingredients. Mix well and allow to draw.

4 Serve Colorful Tortellini Salad garnished with pepper strips and fresh parsley.

**Serves 4**

salt

9 oz/250 g asparagus

7 oz/200 g spinach
spiral pasta

1 bunch radishes

1 bunch fresh chives

2 scallions

3½ oz/100 g smoked
turkey breast

1 tbsp lemon juice

1 tbsp white wine vinegar

2 tbsp sour cream

pepper

*Prep. time: ca. 30 min.*
*(plus cooling time)*
*Per portion ca. 268 kcal/1124 kJ*
*13 g P, 7 g F, 38 g C*

# Spring Salad with Pasta

1  Bring 3 quarts salted water to a boil. Wash the asparagus, cut off the woody end and peel. Cut each stalk in pieces about ¾ in/2 cm long and cook until al dente, about 8 minutes. Remove the asparagus with a slotted spoon, rinse in cold water, and drain.

2  Cook the pasta in the asparagus water according to the package instructions. Pour off the hot water, rinse in cold water, drain well, and allow to cool.

3  Trim, wash, and thinly slice the radishes. Rinse the chives and cut in small rings. Trim and wash the scallions and slice finely. Cut the turkey breast in strips.

4  Mix the lemon juice, vinegar, and sour cream in a bowl. Season to taste with salt and pepper. Thoroughly combine all of the ingredients with the dressing and serve.

# Green Pasta Salad

Cook the pasta in ample salted water until al dente, ...rding to the package instructions.

Wash the peas, cut off the tips and blanch briefly in boiling ...er. Pour off the hot water, rinse under cold water, and drain.

Trim, wash, deseed and dice the red pepper. Trim and wash scallions, then slice into fine rings. Wash the herbs, shake them ... and mince.

4 Drain the macaroni. Thoroughly blend the yoghurt, cream, and horseradish and season to taste with salt and pepper.

5 Combine the dressing with the vegetables, then add the pasta and coat it well. Serve Green Pasta Salad just slightly warm.

**Serves 4**
9 oz/250 g
elbow macaroni
salt
3½ oz/100 g
sugar snap peas
1 red pepper
1 bunch scallions
½ bunch fresh dill
½ bunch fresh basil
1 bunch flat-leaf parsley
4 tbsp yoghurt
4 tbsp cream
1 tbsp horseradish
pepper

*Prep. time: ca. 30 min.*
*Per portion ca. 255 kcal/1071 kJ*
*10 g P, 2 g F, 48 g C*

# Asparagus Noodle Salad

1 Break the tagliatelle in pieces before adding it and the oil to ...oiling salted water and cooking it until al dente. Pour off the hot ...ater, rinse in cold water, then let drain.

2 Cut the turkey breast in strips. Drain the asparagus and ...reserve the liquid.

3 Mix the salad dressing with a bit of asparagus liquid and season to taste with salt, pepper, and paprika. Combine the salad ingredients with the dressing and allow to draw.

4 Serve the salad garnished with fresh lemon balm leaves.

**Serves 4**
7 oz/200 g tagliatelle
1 tsp oil
salt
7 oz/200 g smoked
turkey breast
1 can asparagus pieces
7 tbsp/100 g
yoghurt salad dressing
pepper
paprika
lemon balm to garnish

*Prep. time: ca. 15 min.*
*Per portion ca. 307 kcal/1280 kJ*
*19 g P, 9 g F, 37 g C*

## Colorful Pasta Salad

**Serves 4**

¾ lb/350 g tagliatelle

salt

3 carrots

2½ tbsp/20 g butter

2 cups/300 g frozen peas

6 tbsp vegetable broth

pepper

1–2 tbsp lemon juice

3 tbsp cider vinegar

4 tbsp olive oil

½ bunch parsley, chopped

7 oz/200 g Gorgonzola

*Prep. time: ca. 20 min.*
*(plus cooling time)*
*Per portion ca. 643 kcal/2699 kJ*
*27 g P, 27 g F, 72 g C*

1 Cook the tagliatelle in ample salted water until al dente, according to package instructions.

2 Wash and peel the carrots, cut them lengthwise into thin strips, then in small pieces. Heat the butter in a large pan and sauté the carrots over low heat for 3 minutes. Add the peas and pour in the vegetable broth. Cover the pan and simmer for 5 minutes. Season to taste with salt, pepper, and the lemon juice.

3 Drain the pasta, rinse in cold water, and let it drain and cool. Mix the vinegar, salt, and pepper for the salad dressing. Whisking constantly, gradually add the olive oil. Wash, dry, and finely chop the parsley, then add it to the salad dressing. Combine the tagliatelle with the vegetables and dressing.

4 Break the Gorgonzola in pieces. Sprinkle the cheese over the salad and serve.

# esh Pasta Salad

Cook the pasta in lightly salted water until al dente, ...ding to the package instructions.

Wash the tomatoes and cut them in narrow wedges. Wash ...pepper, cut it in half, remove the seeds, and cut the flesh in ...s. Cut the cheese in strips as well.

When it is cooked, pour the hot water off the pasta, rinse ...cold water, then drain well and allow to cool. Trim, wash, and ...p the celery.

4 Combine the pasta and vegetables in a salad bowl. Whisk together the Italian herbs, olive oil, and vinegar. Season the dressing to taste with salt, pepper and paprika.

5 Pour the dressing over the salad ingredients, mix well, and allow to draw for about 10 minutes before serving.

**Serves 4**

9 oz/250 g spaghetti
salt
3½ oz/100 g
cherry tomatoes
1 yellow pepper
5 oz/150 g Emmentaler
(Swiss) cheese
4 celery stalks
3½ oz/100 g chopped
Italian herbs (e.g., basil,
oregano, thyme, parsley)
½ cup/125 ml olive oil
4 tbsp cider vinegar
pepper
paprika

*Prep. time: ca. 35 min.*
*Per portion ca. 631 kcal/2651 kJ*
*8 g P, 6 g F, 14 g C*

# Recipe Index